Advance Praise

"The words in this bo[...] to attack each day [...] optimism I need to liv[...]

— **Vernon Davis**, Super Bowl Champion, Actor, Philanthropist, and Entrepreneur

"Stress is something we all experience, but what we may not realize is how much it's holding us back. Dr. E's newest book will inspire you to take a look inside yourself and address your problems at their source, allowing you to have the best career and relationships possible!"

— **Rachel DeAlto**, Author of *relatable: How to Connect with Anyone Anywhere (Even if It Scares You)*

"In today's environment, it is very easy to be hijacked by fear, anger, and anxiety. These moments can cost us dearly in professional opportunities, relationships, and happiness. Dr. E's research-driven approach breaks down the obstacles you face in your day-to-day life to help you perform at the highest level and achieve exceptional results."

— **Stephen Drum**, Retired Navy SEAL Master Chief

"My podcast, *Better Together w/ Anne & Heather,* and our tribe of listeners depend on Dr. E each month for her concrete tips to living a happier life. Her latest book, *Get out of the Red Zone*, highlights her concept that I now live by: recognize when you are in a red zone. If you don't know what I am talking about, you must read this book!"

— **Anne Heche**, Emmy Award-winning Actor and Activist

"Is stress leading you to scream at your kids, reach for that fattening doughnut, or say or do things you regret? In these pages, Dr. Lombardo will show you how to get out of the "Red Zone" and how to be calm, happy, and in control no matter how stressful life gets. If you're ready to take your life back—and to make the most of every single day—this is a must-read."

– **Dr. Kellyann Petrucci**, NYT bestselling Author, *Dr. Kellyann's Bone Broth Diet*, Host of the PBS special *21 Days to a Slimmer, Younger You*, and Creator of drkellyann.com

"*Get Out of the Red Zone* acknowledges an important truth: We are often our own greatest obstacles when it comes to achieving success. This book teaches you how to stop self-sabotaging to reach your full potential!"

– **Ellen Rogin**, Co-Author of the New York Times Bestseller *Picture Your Prosperity*

"Powerful and timely! Dr. Elizabeth Lombardo's book, *Get Out of the Red Zone* offers a compelling new model for transforming stress into an authentic breakthrough of the next greatest version of yourself. In these pages are a step by step roadmap and tools for those who desire to do their inner work and thus awaken personal and professional peak potential. Dr. Lombardo gives our mind a reason to accept what our heart intuitively knows . . . love is the great healer of life and the power to move through the Red Zone is an act of self-love. This book is a "must" for any library of science and healing for the 21st century!"

– **Darren R Weissman DC**, Author - *The Power of Infinite Love & Gratitude, Awakening to the Secret Code of Your Mind, The Heart of the Matter*, and Developer of The LifeLine Technique®

GET OUT OF THE RED ZONE

RED ZONE

TRANSFORM YOUR STRESS
AND OPTIMIZE **TRUE SUCCESS**™

ELIZABETH LOMBARDO, PHD

INSPIREBYTES OMNI MEDIA

Get Out of The Red Zone:
Transform Your Stress and Optimize TRUE SUCCESS™

Distributed globally with Expanded Distribution by KDP.

ISBN Paperback: 978-1-953445-07-0
ISBN E-Book: 978-1-953445-20-9
Library of Congress Control Number: 2021944726

⬚ INSPIREBYTES OMNI MEDIA

Inspirebytes Omni Media LLC
PO Box 988
Wilmette, IL 60091

For more information, please visit www.inspirebytes.com.

To Jeffrey, Kelly, Grace, and Bailey—
for helping me remember
every day what is truly important.

Table of Contents

Introduction

It's bizarre. When a stranger sits down next to a medical doctor on a plane or at a dinner party, they often share stories about broken bones or illnesses. They might even ask for an off-the-cuff diagnosis.

My experience has been quite the opposite. When I'm introduced as Dr. E, the psychologist, strangers often become uncomfortable, sharing comments like, "I hope you're not psychoanalyzing me." Many even confess to being worried I'll discover something is wrong with them.

I always laugh at this because I'm not that kind of psychologist. Sure, I have a Ph.D. in clinical psychology, but I don't work with clients on the proverbial "shrink's couch."

I work with highly successful, talented people. Athletes, executives, and Fortune 500 companies count on me to help them optimize their already productive lives. Most of my days are spent presenting keynote speeches, coaching clients, leading workshops, or hosting executive roundtables. I'm a regular contributor to media outlets such as *The Today Show, Good Morning America, Dr. Oz, Forbes*, and *The New York Times*.

I'm in my sweet spot helping ambitious, talented, smart people reach new heights of personal and professional achievement. In a former career, I was a physical therapist and fitness instructor. My natural curiosity and drive led me to learn more about how to maximize the body's potential. Then I discovered the wonders of psychology and how the brain can be harnessed to reach new heights. Now, I work with celebrities, entrepreneurs, and executives to help them find "true success"—the flow that happens when we experience authentic **passion**, **purpose**, and positive relationships with **people**.

I even have a patented, proven formula for better living that I call the True Success™ formula. I'll tell you more about that later.

Abundance Mentality

A foundational aspect of this formula for success is **passion**—defined (by me) as **positive energy, even during difficult times**. While many people believe that the acquisition of money and power diminishes stress, in fact, the opposite is true. The key is not eliminating stress, but rather learning to manage it in order to transform it. Fortunately, I've spent decades researching and studying ways to do this. That research comes in handy in my own life on a daily basis.

The greatest challenge my clients face isn't a lack of knowledge or resources—more often, it's an *abundance* of distress. In spite of resources and opportunities, they get overwhelmed and act out in ways that are inconsistent with who they are at their core—they're in the Red Zone. And I get it. I can totally relate, because I've been there.

Why I'm a Believer

As I write this, my husband—my best friend and partner for over half my life—is very ill. He has been on a ventilator for the past four years requiring around-the-clock care. His health has been slowly declining due to

ALS, and his prognosis is very poor. Sadly, our two daughters bear witness to this horrific deterioration on a daily basis, since, according to conventional medicine, there is no cure.

To say this is a stressful experience would be a severe understatement. To witness my beloved partner's body becoming weaker and weaker can easily throw me into a Red Zone of helplessness, sadness, and fear.

While there are times when I am in the Red Zone (I am human, after all), the majority of my life is good. In fact, overall, I am happy. It's hard knowing that my husband is dying, but I still get to be with him, which makes me happy. I also get to be close with my daughters, and I get to work with clients and pursue my purpose and passion.

I don't deny what is happening in my life. And it doesn't make me a heartless person to be happy—I simply practice what I preach. And I want to help YOU feel happier, more positive, and empowered, no matter what is happening in your life.

If you long to experience a happier, healthier life, with greater success and fulfillment with fewer episodes of distress, this book is for you.

Even if you can't see it yet, there's a bigger and more powerful version of you on the inside, ready to shine. Regardless of what's going on now or what happened in your past, YOU can bring your light out to reach your fullest potential.

It's time to leave the Red Zone behind and discover a life of true passion and True Success™! There's no time like the present. Let's get started.

Chapter One

The
Red Zone

"What's wrong with me? Am I a bad person?"

Silas sat across from me and ran his hands through his hair, clearly distressed.[1] "I keep going over and over it in my head, but it's like I'm watching someone else's life. I mean, who does something like that? My family means everything to me." He shook his head.

"Tell me more," I prompted.

"It's just that it had been the longest day. This new acquisition at work has my team in knots—we're working our tails off. Lara made some remark about me being home late again for dinner, and I don't know, I lost it,"

"Lost it how?"

"I threw a glass. It shattered into a million pieces. My kids sat there—they looked at me like they didn't know me. I was mortified, Dr. E! When I think of how someone could have been hurt…," his voice broke. "All I know is, that's not me. I never want to feel that way again. I need help."

Silas was normally a rational, pleasant, and upstanding citizen. He ran a successful start-up company. He was an athlete, in great shape, and had a strong support system. What was going on? Had aliens taken over his body? Was he having a nervous breakdown?

As a psychologist, I hear stories like this a lot. When our actions don't line up with who we know we are inside, it can be confusing and upsetting. This feeling only adds to the pressure that triggered the outburst in the first place.

Silas was experiencing what I call the psychological Red Zone. We've all spent time there, whether we admit it or not.

The Red Zone is not a physical space. It's a head-space—a frame of mind.

Certainly, we've all witnessed co-workers, family, friends, neighbors, and even strangers in the Red Zone.

- The co-worker who bursts into tears in a business meeting.
- The family member who screams at the kids while preparing a festive holiday meal.
- The friend who "lets you have it" for a perceived slight.
- The neighbor who leaves a nasty voicemail complaining about your dog.

Red Zone incidents make for great headlines. They're captivating precisely because they're so bewildering, such as an argument between a celebrity couple at a restaurant or the athlete who stormed the paparazzi. We wonder, "What in the world is going on there?"

Confessions From the Red Zone

I'm no stranger to the Red Zone. Like the time I gave a keynote speech at a big conference in San Francisco.

Determined to be home in Chicago in time for breakfast with my two daughters, I took the last flight back east. That trip took longer than expected due to a three-hour weather delay. When the plane finally touched down at O'Hare, I was exhausted—but relieved. I wanted to crawl into bed.

Our house was dark when I arrived. When I walked through my front door, I practically tripped over bookbags, shoes, and coats my daughters had left on the floor where they had, apparently, dropped everything after school. I was livid. A peek inside my mind at that moment would look something like this: *I work all day and bust my butt to get home to try to be a good mother, and they can't even take 30 seconds to put their stuff away. Why do I even bother when they're so disrespectful?!*

I was furious and energized—suddenly not a bit sleepy. I threw their bags into the closet, did a load of laundry, and wrote a long speech in my head that I was determined to deliver the moment they woke up for school. Then I caught a glimpse of myself in the mirror. My expression reminded me of the Incredible Hulk.

What was going on here? Finding bookbags laying on the floor was nothing new in our house. When it had happened in the past, I calmly and assertively reminded my girls about their responsibilities to put away their things. So in essence, the same thing had happened before, and I hadn't lost my cool.

So what was the difference? My reaction this time was completely different when I got home from California. Why?

I was in the Red Zone. It wasn't pretty. It wasn't productive. And, most importantly, it didn't engender love and growth in my relationships with my daughters.

I wished for a do-over.

"Never Have I Ever"

Maybe this scene feels familiar to you, or perhaps your Red Zone looks completely different. We've all been there in one way or another.

In the "Never Have I Ever" game, players answer revealing questions. It's like Truth or Dare, with a twist. The following quick checklist is a bit like that, but with the added component of doctor-patient (er, make that "reader") confidentiality. Answer with a nod or silence.

Never Have I Ever…

- Said something I later regretted
- Consumed something I wish I hadn't
- Gotten really upset about something, only to later realize it wasn't that big of a deal
- Procrastinated on an important task
- "Lost it" on someone
- Had trouble focusing or concentrating
- Gotten defensive
- Been told to "Just calm down" (advice that is rarely helpful)

If you nodded even once, please know that (a) you were probably in the Red Zone, and (b) you are human. Being in the Red Zone is something we have all experienced and is absolutely normal. The thing is: it stinks. More importantly, though, nobody wants to be there.

The Zone of True Success™

Sometimes I wish there was a remote control for my life. If I had one, I would have used it to hit rewind during the wee hours of the morning after my trip home from California. I'd have gone back to six hours before I slipped into the Red Zone, when I was in the Zone of True Success™. I was thriving! Speaking in San Francisco at that event was exhilarating, challenging, and fun. When I'm passionate about something—drawing on my experience and expertise—it's like a beautiful symphony. My thoughts, beliefs, and behaviors are all in sync. Some people call this "flow." It feels good. I'm expending energy, but I'm also generating it. I feel like Goldilocks did when she said, "It's just right." I feel authentically me, aligned, and purposeful.

That's the goal, isn't it? We want to feel that productive energy as much and as often as possible. We want to feel that passion—positive energy, even during difficult times. Understanding the Red Zone can help get you there.

Power of the Red Zone

The purpose of this book is to introduce you to the concept of the Red Zone so that you can understand its power and then take control of it, rather than letting it control you. All that energy is real. It can be destructive, or it can be productive.

Mastering the Red Zone is pivotal to success. This skill will impact every important area of your life: work, health, finances, goal-setting, romance, relationships. Because once we understand the Red Zone, we're free to choose to leave it and discover a better way.

In this book, I'll teach you how and why the Red Zone can take over your thoughts and reactions, and I'll give you the tools and skills to get out of the Red Zone to experience True Success™.

Let's start by looking at what it really is.

Where Is This Red Zone?

The Red Zone is not really a place; it's a state of being where heightened stress tips a person out of alignment. How the Red Zone shows up is unique to each individual, but it's defined by high levels of distress. In psychology, we use the term "distress" to encompass pretty much any feeling you don't want: anger, frustration, fear, worry, sadness, overwhelm, guilt, shame, embarrassment, hopelessness, helplessness, worthlessness, etc. Yuck!

Distress exists on a continuum. Consider: What does it feel like to be angry? Sometimes we feel mildly irritated (a little angry) or so angry we start yelling, throwing something, or get so enraged we can barely see. There are different levels of anger, just like there are different levels of physical pain.

Any negative feeling of distress falls on a continuum from zero to ten. A zero would basically mean "no distress at all," and a ten out of ten would be the most distressed you have ever been.

This means that on a scale of sadness, a three out of ten may mean you feel somewhat bummed. In contrast, a ten out of ten might result in crying, and not just a cute tear glistening down your cheek, but rather snot-coming-out-of-your-nose sobbing.

Most of us don't spend a lot of time at ten, and probably aren't at a zero all the time either. Usually, we are somewhere in between.

So consider:

- Right now, where is your distress level?
- How about when you first wake up in the morning?
- When you go to work or start your day?
- When you interact with that difficult person in your life?
- When your workday is over, and you are starting with the next phase of your day?
- Before you go to sleep?

When you're a seven or higher on the scale of distress, you reach the Red Zone. When we are in the Red Zone, we are usually not thinking 100% rationally.

You probably notice that your level of distress fluctuates throughout the day according to the time of day, what you're doing, who you're with, and even your physiology. When we're hungry or tired, for example, stress levels tend to be higher. Being "hangry" is a great example of how our physiology impacts our level of distress.

The reason why this is important is because our level of distress impacts how we view and interact with the world. Specifically, the higher level of distress you have, the more likely you are to see things in an adverse or gloomy way. Distress distorts or impairs our vision.

Have you ever watched an inspiring movie, heard a motivational speech, or learned about someone who has overcome significant odds and thought, "YES! That completely transformed my life. I can do anything!" While that sentiment may have felt 100% true at the time, within a short period of time, we often resume old habits and patterns. Why is that?

Stress zones may play a role.

Mindset and the Red Zone

Traci reached out to me after watching "The Biggest Loser." Her doctor had recommended she lose 80 pounds. "I never thought I could do it," she said. "Then I saw Ali Vincent do it. She actually won! Now I *know* I can. And I want you to help keep me on track."

This was music to my ears. I'm a health and physical fitness enthusiast. In addition to my degree in psychology, I am also a physical therapist. I even taught group fitness for almost 20 years. I know how vitally important mindset is when it comes to improving health, especially with something like losing weight.

When we first chatted, Traci's distress was low and her enthusiasm was high. She was in the Green Zone, where distress is at 0–3/10. But by the time we met the following week, her "high" had worn off. "I almost didn't come in today," Traci shared during our first session. "I don't know what I was thinking before. I'm embarrassed. There's no way I can lose all this weight."

As we explored her mindset, I asked what her current level of distress was. "A seven, at least." And what was her typical distress level when she was binge eating? "Definitely a nine or ten."

Where you are on the distress scale can significantly impact how you view yourself, your situation, and others. We will explore more about why that is in a bit. For now, let's look at Green versus Red Zone experiences.

Green Zone (Distress level 0–3/10)	Red Zone (Distress level 7–10/10)
"I am in charge of how I feel/ act today, regardless of what has happened or is happening."	"I am a victim of the past."
"He's having a bad day."	"He disrespected me!"
"This is a setback. But there are upsides, too."	"This is horrible."
"He may not love me, but I have friends and family who do."	"Nobody loves me."
"I choose to be more assertive in asking for assistance."	"I have to do everything myself."
"I mess up sometimes; I am human."	"I am a loser."
"I can do this. I can feel it in me."	"Who do I think I am? I can't do that."
"I am valuable and I add value."	"I am worthless."

Can you relate to experiencing both Green and Red Zone thoughts? Most people can. And no, it's not because you have multiple personalities or that you are "bipolar," as one client feared. The difference can be found in the level of distress you are currently experiencing.

Limbic Hijack = Pessimism

Ever notice how when you're really upset, you tend to view people and events in a more negative light? What people do or say can cause you more distress, even if it's something they do or say often. Presumably "little" events can feel like colossal experiences.

Most of rational human thought goes on in the frontal lobe, which is the structure in the brain that differentiates humans from other animals.[2] It allows us to engage in problem-solving, to see other people's perspectives, and to use executive functioning. When distress is low, the frontal lobe is hard at work. So under low-stress conditions, we're likely to be rational and positive.

When distress comes into play, however, the limbic system is activated, overriding the frontal lobe. The limbic system is an area in the "lower" part of your brain. It's responsible for fight-or-flight and emotional reasoning. So when the limbic system is activated, instead of processing information rationally using your frontal lobe, the brain processes the information in more pessimistic ways—in essence, attempting to survive as if under threat of extinction. While this is helpful if you're actually in a life-threatening situation, it's not the kind of thinking that helps a person thrive long-term.

The higher-level distress you have, the less reasonable you probably are. You're less likely to see different perspectives, and you're more likely to focus on the negative (i.e., what's wrong with the person, situation, you…), feel stuck, and personalize others' actions.

If someone speaks to you in a gruff manner when you're at a low level of distress, you are likely to brush it off. "He must be tired," or, "She's having a bad day," might be your interpretation. When you're in the Red Zone, though, the same tone might provoke a defensive, insulted, or even irate response.

Think about a time when you were *really* distressed. Perhaps you were angry at a loved one, hurt by a colleague's comments, or worried about something bad happening. At the time, your reasons for feeling like that made a lot of sense to you. They were based on what you thought was the absolute truth. But later, after some time had passed and you didn't feel so upset, you could see how there might have been another side to the story.

Fallout From the Red Zone

Consider Michael and Julie. They came to see me for couples counseling. Working together as a couple with a therapist or coach can be very helpful at certain points of a relationship to strengthen communication and love. Unfortunately, people often wait until it's too late to try couples counseling—when one person is already "out of the relationship" in their mind, despite not openly communicating that to their partner.

Luckily, Michael and Julie had not gotten to that point. They had been struggling with their marriage since the birth of their son, Kyle, six months earlier.

The night/morning before one of our sessions, they had a huge argument. Kyle was still not sleeping through the whole night, resulting in severe sleep deprivation for both of his parents. Around 2am, he let out a loud shriek. Both parents just wanted to go back to sleep. Julie usually got up in the middle of the night (she had taken an extended maternity leave) but was too exhausted to move. Michael had a big meeting for work the next day. At first, they both laid there, hoping the other person would jump up to take care of their son.

That did not happen.

Eventually, Julie got up, yelled at Michael for being a bad father, and went to take care of Kyle. Thirty minutes later, after getting Kyle settled and back to sleep, she woke Michael up (annoyed he was snoring) and shared her opinion of him even more. Michael started yelling and trying to defend himself, "I have a meeting with the board tomorrow. I can't fall asleep during it." It was a mess. They were both in the Red Zone.

During our therapy session, after they were both out of the Red Zone, we explored what happened. "I don't really think you are a bad dad, Michael," Julie communicated. "I'm just exhausted."

Any parent can relate to this scenario. Really, if you have ever been sleep deprived or exhausted for any reason, you can probably empathize with Julie's Red Zone reaction.

From Julie's example, we can see how, in the Red Zone, we view the world differently. We are more likely to see the negative, personalize other people's actions, and become a victim of our circumstances. Not only does that feel lousy, it also impacts our relationships because it affects our interactions with others.

What's more, being in the Red Zone can impact pretty much every facet of your life. Here are some common consequences of being in the Red Zone:

Emotional Well-Being:

- Anger, resentment
- Guilt, shame
- Sadness, crying
- Anxiety, worry

Mental Functioning:

- Lack of focus
- Difficulty concentrating
- Problems with memory

Physical Health:

- Difficulty sleeping
- Eating more or making unhealthy food choices
- Avoiding exercise or engaging in excessive exercise
- Unexplained physical pain, such as headaches, neck/back pain, gastrointestinal distress

Relationships:

- Personalizing what others are doing or saying
- Being easily offended

- Being irritable with others
- Yelling
- "Clamming up" and not openly communicating
- Being passive-aggressive
- Blaming others

Work:

- Procrastination
- Difficulty making decisions (sometimes referred to as "analysis paralysis")
- Problems staying on task
- Spending time on unnecessary tasks and avoiding what is most important
- Not going to work
- Performing suboptimally because of issues with mental functioning
- Making more mistakes
- Increase in work-related injuries

Spirituality:

- Lack of purpose
- Focus on self versus helping others

The Hidden Cost of the Red Zone

The Red Zone isn't just an individual's issue. It can also be a corporate issue. The Red Zone is about distress, and we know from reams of research that stress costs U.S. companies over $300 billion annually. Stress is cited as the source of most absenteeism, "presenteeism" (when employees are "there" but not really working), poor engagement, employee turnover, and healthcare utilization. As CNBC reported, "Supporting workers with mental health services is not only an ethical obligation for employers, it's also a bottom-line issue."[3]

Particularly since the COVID-19 pandemic, my company has been helping organizations train employees on getting out of the Red Zone. I love teaching clients about our amazing ability to control our level of distress. It's so powerful to see the transformations individuals and teams make when they learn and apply these skills. Clients report that after training, their teams are more focused, engaged, and proactive—which translates to the bottom line.

With fewer incidents of employees in the Red Zone, companies are more efficient, creative, and productive. Less distress can translate into greater happiness. Research out of Harvard University, for example, illustrates the impact of happiness on business. Happier employees enjoy:[4]

- 15 fewer sick days/year
- 19% increase in accuracy
- 31% increase in productivity
- 37% increase in sales
- 40% increase in promotions
- 40% decrease in health-related costs

It's clear that learning to get out of the Red Zone benefits all concerned.

Taking Back Control

I want to help you stay out of the Red Zone so you can experience more passion—positive energy, even during difficult times. So let's explore what puts us in the Red Zone in the first place and learn some specific steps we can take to avoid getting into that truly heightened state of distress. But first, we need to learn how to recognize the Red Zone.

Chapter Two

Check Engine Lights: Mental, Physical, & Behavioral Cues That You're in the Red Zone

Dave came to see me at the insistence of his wife, Vanessa. "She thinks I have anger management issues," he shared in our first meeting.

"And what do you think?" I asked.

He proceeded to share with me that after a long day of work, which tended to be most weekdays, he would come home to his wife and three children. "I love them all so much," he said, "I really do. And I know Vanessa has been with them all day and needs a break. I really want to give her that break, but sometimes I just lose it on the kids. I get upset because one of them spills their milk all over the table during dinner, or they are splashing around in the bath instead of getting clean. I'm embarrassed to even say this out loud. I don't even realize how irritated I am until I'm yelling at the kids. Maybe I do have anger management issues."

Actually, in my assessment, Dave had Red Zone management issues.

Has that ever happened to you? Maybe you behaved in a way that you later determined was an overreaction, without realizing you were in the Red Zone?

Maybe you had an experience where you overreacted. Something little turned out to be the proverbial "straw that broke the camel's back."

When you're experiencing high levels of distress, one event can bump you into the Red Zone.

While we've established that the Red Zone takes place when we are at a seven out of ten or higher on the distress scale, sometimes we're not cognizant that we're actually in it until we've reacted in ways that don't align with who we want to be, and then we feel awful.

It's funny. Cars come equipped with tones that remind us to fasten seat belts and lights that indicate "tire pressure is low." Such signals equip us to handle normal or even tough driving conditions. Wouldn't it be nice if we had a dashboard with lights that indicate, "Warning! You're entering the Red Zone!"

Red Flags

The fact is, our bodies *are* equipped with such signals! We just need to learn to recognize these "Red Flags" that let us know when we are in the Red Zone. These indicators include: emotions, physical sensations, and behaviors. Let's dig into all three.

Emotions

When we feel unpleasant emotions, they often indicate distress. This could be heightened by:

- Sadness
- Fear
- Worry

- Anxiety
- Guilt
- Shame
- Anger
- Disappointment
- Jealousy
- Disgust
- Loneliness
- Loathing
- Helplessness
- Hopelessness
- Worthlessness

A lot of people have their "go to" emotions when they're in the Red Zone. Some tend to feel angry while others may feel sad or anxious.

Think about times when you were recently in the Red Zone. What mental feelings did you experience?

Physical Sensations

We often think of unpleasant physical sensations as symptoms of illness. In fact, physical sensation Red Flags are often our bodies' reaction to distress. These can include:

- Headache
- Back pain
- Neck pain
- Tight muscles

- Nausea
- Butterflies in your stomach
- Sweating
- Feeling hot or cold
- Tightness in your chest
- Chronic pain

While any of these symptoms could be your immune system at work (for example, you might feel nauseous because you have a stomach virus), if you are not ill, it's important to also ask yourself why you might be experiencing this physical sensation.

I remember when I was working on my dissertation defense. I had conducted a year-long psychology research study and was writing up the results that I would then present to my dissertation committee. Along with the few months left of my internship, getting a "pass" from the committee was the only thing keeping me from obtaining my Ph.D. As a result, I was feeling quite stressed out.

One day, I walked by the mirror and noticed that my shoulders were practically connected to my ears. I hadn't realized it before, but I was experiencing incredible tightness in my neck as a result of feeling so overwhelmed.

What's more, chronic distress can lead to health issues. There is a field of study called "psychoneuroimmunology" (or "PNI") that studies the relationship between psychology (stress), the nervous system, and the immune system. People who experience prolonged stress (i.e., being in the Red Zone) are more susceptible to illness because their immune system is negatively impacted, making it harder to fight off infections. Wound healing is also influenced by levels of stress. For example, one study found that caregivers (who are often under an enormous amount of stress) took an average of 24% longer to heal a small, standardized wound than matched controls.[5]

So for you, how does your body feel when you are in the Red Zone, or experiencing elevated levels of distress?

Behaviors

When it comes to behavioral Red Flags, these could be things that you do or say, as well as things you don't do or say. They can include:

- Yelling or being terse
- Fidgeting behaviors
- Overeating or not eating
- Consuming more "comfort food" and/or making less healthy choices
- Increased consumption of alcohol
- Use of drugs
- Procrastinating
- Closing up or not speaking with others
- Avoiding people or social situations
- Avoiding time to yourself
- Difficulty focusing
- Poor performance at work
- Making someone else "wrong" or putting them down

Humans in the Red Zone are not thinking or behaving in a way that is 100% rational. I always tell my coaching clients, "If you're at a seven or higher on the distress scale, don't let anything out of your mouth (because that's when we say things we regret). And don't let anything into your mouth (because that's when we tend to consume things that we don't necessarily want)." This is a good guideline to seriously consider.

Each of us has our own list of "go-to" behaviors when we are experiencing heightened levels of distress. Take some time to consider what you do or say—or don't do or say—when you are in the Red Zone.

Observations of Others That Signal the Red Zone

Red Flags can be self-identified; you might notice that what you are feeling and doing is out of character. However, this isn't always the case. As in the case of Michael and Julie, we may not be aware of our own Red Flags, whereas those around us are.

I work with a lot of executives to help them cultivate their skills as leaders. Great leadership, you see, starts from the inside out. One particular executive initially wanted nothing to do with me. During our first meeting, Jay blurted out, "I'm fine! I don't need this! I don't have time for you!" I was able to share with Jay that though he didn't recognize the signs, his team did. There had been numerous complaints about his irritability and disrespect. Jay needed to learn to recognize and navigate his way out of the Red Zone. Once he heard me and accepted the observations of others (which took a little time!), he was receptive. With some training, Jay found himself much happier and more productive, and so were his team members. What's more, Jay eventually shared the concept of getting out of the Red Zone with his colleagues, who then started applying it in their lives, too.

Sometimes, others can see clearly what we can't see for ourselves.

What feedback are you receiving from others? What kinds of feedback do you get from family, friends, and colleagues about your emotions, your behaviors, your mood, and your interactions?

This is not a time to judge or shame yourself or others. Rather, it's an opportunity for honesty and growth. Others' feedback can be the catalyst you need for positive change.

The Gift of Discomfort

As we look at how distress shows up for you, it's important to realize emotional discomfort can be a good thing because it provides key information about what is going on.

There is a rare disorder called Congenital Insensitivity to Pain (CIP) where a person's ability to feel pain is inhibited. Whether it's a papercut on their finger, a sprained ankle, or a broken arm—none of these physical ailments can be felt. While some may think, "Wow, I wish I could never feel pain," in reality, pain can be a good thing. Human survival depends on it. Unfortunately, most people with this disorder don't survive past the age of 25.

Why? Because pain tells you when something is wrong. It tells you where you need to focus your attention.

The sensation of pain makes us aware that something harmful is happening so that we can take steps to stop the injury and promote healing. That pain is a gift—it helps us know something is not right and that we need to do something about it.

When someone with CIP touches a hot stove, they don't feel the burn. As a result, they're not prompted to move their hand away, resulting in a more severe burn. Certainly, that is not healthy.

Though this particular condition is rare, I personally witnessed a similar condition that is more prevalent. A common symptom for people with diabetes is neuropathy, or a dysfunction in their peripheral nerves. Sometimes this can present as increased pain (such as a burning sensation), and other times it can create a lack of pain perception. When I was a practicing physical therapist, one of the methods I always shared with my clients with diabetes was a skin check, especially of the feet.

I once worked with a client who had rather severe diabetes. When conducting a skin check, we found a thumbtack stuck in the bottom of his foot. I have no idea how long he had been walking on the tack, but the damage to the area was significant. In fact, it was so severe that the client ended up requiring a partial surgical foot amputation to prevent the infection from spreading into his leg and other parts of the body, which could have literally become life threatening. His diabetic neuropathy functioned like CIP and completely prevented him from feeling pain, which worsened the situation.

In the right circumstances, pain can be good and necessary. Pain offers us insights into what's going on when we use it as biofeedback.

Distress also offers us a biofeedback signal. Except rather than something being "off" physically, distress alerts us to the potential that something is "off" mentally.

That's why it's important to see Red Flags as helpful and not harmful in and of themselves.

Pain as a Path to Healing

Lucinda initially came to see me because of my success in helping clients deal with chronic pain. She was experiencing debilitating headaches. When we first started working together, Lucinda described her husband of fifteen years as the love of her life and her career as the job of her dreams. As we began really exploring what was going on in her life, we took note of when her headaches occurred. She reported that they often came on at the end of a long workday when she came home and felt exhausted. This seemed reasonable. A long, stressful day can induce a headache.

What was interesting to me was that when Lucinda traveled for work, working even longer days, she experienced no headaches. In fact, she reported her pain at a zero out of ten even on the most hectic days of traveling.

So what was happening? Well, with further searching, we uncovered some disconnect between what she said about her husband and what she was actually experiencing. While he *was* a great person and she felt like she *should* be in love with him, in truth (and this took a lot of digging to uncover, because she didn't want to admit it, even to herself), she was really conflicted about her marriage. She felt excruciating guilt because she had pursued him for years. And while she was trying to act as if everything was great, that she was living the life of her dreams, deep down, she knew it was a farce. The cognitive dissonance manifested as a physical Red Flag: severe headaches.

After we'd worked together for a while, Lucinda was able to make some positive changes for both her and her husband. She shared with her husband what was going on with her, and he admitted that he felt similarly. They ended up divorcing, and both found the true loves of their lives. The last I heard, she had been living with her new partner, pain free, for over six months.

Having taken note of the Red Flag that indicated that something was going on, she was able to act to stop the pain and begin to heal. The biofeedback was initially uncomfortable but ultimately led to healing. Had she ignored it, she would not have taken the steps she needed to truly create the life she loves.

Beliefs About Biofeedback

My happiest and most successful clients have learned this critical distinction: Discomfort isn't something to be avoided—it's a gift. We need to learn to perceive emotional, physical, and behavioral biofeedback as exactly what it is: a Red Flag or dashboard signal designed to point us toward healing and happiness.

Chapter Three

What Causes You to Go Into the Red Zone?

What causes the distress we have been exploring?

When I ask my clients what causes them distress, they can often readily cite a list of external circumstances—things that happen *to* them. These myriad "causes" can almost always be classified into two categories: people and events.

Clients report that what people say or do—or what they *don't* say or *don't* do—results in anger, worry, sadness, shame, and other negative feelings. They also cite events (such as not getting the promotion, the traffic, the excessive meetings) that instigate distress.

It may surprise you to hear that neither people nor events actually cause distress. What is responsible for it? The mediator variable.

The Mediator Variable

When I use this term, I often see puzzled looks on my clients' faces. Some may recall this term from college or graduate classes. After all, it's a term frequently used in statistics courses. Over the course of my own education, I took a few statistics courses (rather reluctantly, I admit). While these weren't my favorite courses, the concept of mediation intrigued me, and it turns out that this term has beautiful implications for human psychology.

A mediation model explains the effect a mediator variable has on the relationship between two variables: an independent variable and a dependent variable. The mediator variable is the factor that determines the impact the independent variable has on the dependent variable, thereby increasing the potential of reaching a specific outcome.

For example, during the COVID-19 pandemic, many joked about "Quarantine 15," which referred to the amount of weight people were likely to gain during the stay-at-home order.

In this case, the independent variable was quarantine (or being stuck at home). The dependent variable, so-called because it's dependent on the quarantine, was the weight gain.

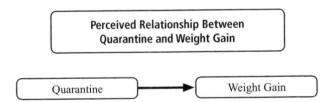

While the "Quarantine 15" was a bit of a joke, it prompted a serious question: Does being in quarantine necessarily *cause* weight gain? Of course not. Many people actually lost weight during this period. Instead, a third variable served as the mediator, or the proverbial fork in the road. What was this variable? The healthy choices they chose or did not choose, also known as their behavior.

If someone consumed more calories than usual and/or exercised a lot less during quarantine, a weight gain was likely. In contrast, those who ate less or exercised more were more likely to lose weight.

The choices someone made (aka: the mediator variable)—not the quarantine—determined the outcome.

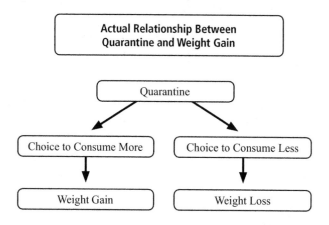

Slide Projector

Here's another way to think about it. Have you ever seen an old-fashioned slide projector? This machine was fairly simple: a box that projects a beam of light through a photographic slide out and onto a screen. It's similar to a movie projector, but instead of moving pictures, the image is static. Back in the day, friends would share slideshows of their vacations. You'd come home from a trip to sunny Florida, have your pictures developed into slides at the camera store, then set up a slide projector in the living room. A beam of light would shoot out of the slide projector onto a blank wall. Someone would pop the slides in front of the beam so that rather than a simple beam of white light on the wall, we'd see the picture of, say, the Grand Canyon or Uncle Bert in his board shorts at the beach. Change the slide and a different image would be projected on the wall of little Fred building a marvelous sandcastle, and so on.

Imagine if you will that the projector is the activating event, the slide is the mediator, and the image on the wall is the end result. While the beam of light is steady and doesn't change, the image projected on the wall is 100% a result of the slide placed in front of the beam. Don't like seeing a sunburnt Aunt Flo? Change the slide and you change the consequence.

So now that we understand what a mediator is, let's look at why it's important when it comes to being in the Red Zone. Let me introduce you to Ted.

Ted's Talks

My client Ted is an executive sales team leader whose team consists of over 600 people. Ted has glossophobia—a fear of public speaking. It's a common struggle many people experience, even those whose jobs require that they talk in front of large groups.

Ted was responsible for his company's annual sales conference. This meant he had to be on stage speaking for hours. This critical meeting for his team was also a high priority for Ted, personally. His company's financial success hinged on the results. Accordingly, he spent a great deal of time preparing for it. Every year, for months before the conference, Ted experienced distress in anticipation of the event. So in this case, speaking on stage was the activating event (in our analogy, it's the slide projector with its beam of light).

The consequences—feeling anxious, problems sleeping, and irritability—were the dependent variables (in our analogy, the resulting image on the wall, even if it's just a box of white light).

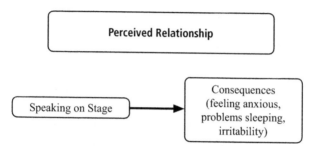

However, it wasn't being on stage, per se, that caused Ted's heightened distress. Instead, it was his beliefs about being on stage that mediated this relationship.

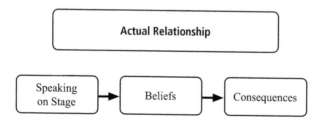

In order to change the consequences, Ted needed to change the slide—the mediator factor. So I asked him to try on two different beliefs.

Belief 1: *I'm going to completely mess up. My team will see that I'm not actually a good speaker. It will be a colossal failure.*

How do you think Ted would react to the "slide" of Belief 1? Well, we know because this was what he was actually thinking. The consequences were more fear, anxiety, and worry. He actually procrastinated on practicing because it caused him so much distress. During the weeks leading up to the sales meeting, he became irritable with his wife and children and suffered from sleepless nights, absorbed with worry.

Now, what if we changed the slide?

Belief 2: *Okay, my heart is racing, and that means I'm excited about this event. I'm so proud of my team and can't wait to celebrate their wins this past year and share some new strategies we're going to implement this coming year.*

What might be the consequences of this belief?

Most likely, Ted would feel enthusiastic about his presentation. He would probably be more upbeat with his family during the weeks before the event and better able to sleep.

Ted put this change into practice and saw an immediate and positive result. His distress levels went from an eight to a three.

While the activating event stayed the same—Ted was still responsible for the annual sales conference—his *belief* changed everything. By changing the "slide," he changed the outcome!

The ABCs of Cause and Effect

Pretty much everything in this life exists in a cause and effect relationship. In psychology, we often refer to this as the ABC model:

A = Activating event

B = Belief/Mediator

C = Consequences (both what someone does and how they feel)

To further understand the middle step in this model, let's look at a powerful example of the mediating role of our thoughts.

Roger was a 42-year-old electrician. One day, Roger was working on a building where the wires were supposed to be inactive. Unfortunately for Roger, the circuit had not been turned off. When he touched the wire, a jolt of electricity surged through his body so intensely that he was knocked unconscious. The electrical burn was so severe that the doctor gave Roger's wife two options: "We can amputate his arms and try to save his life, or let him die."

This was a choice no reasonable person would like to make. Roger's wife didn't want her husband to die, so she elected for a surgical amputation of both of her husband's arms, hoping that it would save his life.

I met Roger when I was doing my postdoctoral training at a major medical center with a Level 1 trauma unit. People who had sustained life-threatening injuries were often brought to this hospital. My role was to help people who had experienced accidents, trauma, significant illness, the death of a loved one, or other misfortunes.

When I first read the consult for Roger, I was at a bit of a loss. I rationalized that Roger was thinking, "I'm a hopeless, helpless, worthless man, and there is nothing I can do." I anticipated that his mindset would cause significant distress and depression, which would also negatively impact his healing and rehab process. Believing "there is nothing I can do" inhibits someone from trying to take steps to make things better. Refusal to participate in physical and occupational therapy prevents someone without arms from learning to function more independently—to eat, dress, and really do any activities of daily living themselves. I was concerned his mindset would also prevent him from taking steps to finding employment or productive and meaningful ways to function in the world.

It was my job to help Roger change his outlook. "But really," I thought as I made my way to Roger's hospital room for the first time, "How am I going to do that?" (I will admit that this is not what you might *want* your psychologist to be thinking, but that was where I was at that point in my career).

Feeling my own distress because of what I *assumed* Roger was experiencing, I knocked on his hospital door and heard a cheerful, "Come in," from the other side. As I entered the room, there was Roger. I'll never forget seeing Roger for the first time. He had a thick head of dark brown hair and a thick brown mustache. He wore the standard bluish-grayish hospital gown and, as expected, had no arms. What I didn't expect was the huge smile on Roger's face.

What's going on here? I thought. *He must be delusional and not realize his arms are gone.*

In reality, I was the one who was delusional. Because, you see, "I'm a hopeless, helpless, worthless man, and there is nothing I can do" was not even remotely Roger's belief.

Roger's belief was, "I'm so grateful that my life has been spared. I *know* I'm still here on this earth for something incredible. I don't know what it is, but I'm excited to figure it out and be on this journey."

How do you think Roger's true beliefs completely changed the trajectory of his life (as compared to the beliefs I assumed he would have)? Roger was genuinely happy and grateful. Yes, he mourned the loss of his limbs, and at the same time, he was hopeful about the future.

Roger exuded a positive energy even during this challenging time, which you now know I define as *passion*. His sense of humor was infectious, his love for his wife almost palpable, and he progressed so quickly that within a few days, he was healing so well that he was transferred to the rehab hospital.

I followed Roger over the course of his rehabilitation— not because he needed me, but because I wanted to see how long this perspective would hold. I was convinced he would slip into a mindset of "I'm a hopeless, helpless, worthless man, and there is nothing I can do." Luckily, I was wrong. His passion persisted. Roger went home with his wife and young son, where he would continue to work with the occupational therapist.

What a difference Roger's thoughts made in terms of his health, recovery, and creating a new life for himself and his family!

What goes on inside our minds is so powerful, and it determines how we interact with the world, including ourselves. Now that we grasp the vital, pivotal role beliefs play in our daily lives, let's look at how we can use this information.

Chapter Four

What Is Your Internal Microphone Picking Up? How to Take Control of Your Thoughts to Create Desired Consequences

As we explored in the last chapter, events alone do not have the power to send us into the Red Zone. They are simply the beam of light pouring out of a projector. Our mediating thoughts determine the outcome, much like the "slides" in the projector. When we change these slides, we can avoid the Red Zone altogether.

Psychiatrist and neurologist Viktor E. Frankl is a personal hero of mine. He witnessed unimaginable horror in concentration camps during World War II, and his book, *Man's Search for Meaning*, has been a foundational work for millions. Having survived the Holocaust, Frankl wrote these profound words:

"Everything can be taken from a man but one thing: the last of human freedoms—to choose one's attitude in any given set of circumstances, to choose one's own way."

Frankl's wisdom is a gift to us, whose lives will (hopefully!) never witness such tragedies again. Building on his message, we know that our thoughts determine our actions and reactions, including how we feel and behave.

What's in the Way?

My client Traci wanted to lose weight. When she looked in the mirror, her inner critic (that little voice inside that shouts mean things) said horrible things to her, like, "You're a fat loser. You will never amount to anything. You've tried so many diets and failed. You're destined to be a failure!"

As you can imagine, these types of thoughts resulted in Traci feeling upset, shame, sadness, and worthlessness. Her thoughts also kept her from taking steps to address her weight, because she believed there was nothing she could do to create a healthy body. As a result, Traci continued with her unhealthy eating habits and avoided exercise.

This is an example of how our thoughts can serve as the mediating variable between the situation and how we react to it.

Words Matter

Now, although we have been talking about thoughts, feelings, and behaviors, it's important that we pause and define these terms, because while they are related, each one is a unique entity.

Behaviors can be defined as what we do or don't do—actions like whispering, yelling, eating ice cream, or walking up stairs. This includes what we say aloud, like, "Excuse me," "Next round's on me!" or, "You're fired!" The category of behaviors also includes willfully choosing *not* to act, such as procrastinating, not brushing your teeth, not answering the phone, or not speaking up. Behaviors are actions that others can see and experience.

Feelings are not obvious to others. You are the only one who knows what you're feeling, for better or worse. Feelings include physical sensations such as pain, muscle tension, or discomfort, as well as emotions, such as sadness, joy, worry, fear, elation, or shame. Again, nobody knows what you're feeling but you (of course, feelings can impact your behaviors, which others *can* see).

Thoughts are basically what you say to yourself. Thoughts can be experienced as either words or images, such as picturing the face of a person who is being discussed or a place where you have traveled before. Most thoughts are not facts, but rather are subjective interpretations. This is key to understanding and getting out of the Red Zone, because while it's our thoughts that propel us into the Red Zone, the majority of those thoughts are not objective truths. Often, thoughts are assumptions or perceptions we've automatically created in our minds without even realizing it! We will explore this more later.

Mood Congruent Thinking

Now that we have the terminology parsed out, let's look at this visually.

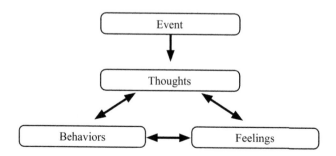

As we previously discussed, thoughts determine feelings and behaviors—it's as simple as ABC. And yet it's more complicated, because these three variables are actually reciprocal and interrelated. In other words, feelings and actions can also impact how we think. Consider: When you feel sad, what kind of thoughts do you have? Probably sad ones. In psychology, we call this "mood congruent thinking." When you feel angry, your thoughts tend to recall other times you were angry. So the relationship between thoughts and feelings actually *goes both ways*.

Similarly, actions can impact thoughts, too. When you do something kind to help out a friend or even a stranger, what kind of thoughts do you have? "That was nice," might resonate in your head. Or when you have a good workout at the gym, you might think, "I'm killing it today!" So it's clear that thoughts and behaviors can impact each other. Again, it's a relationship that goes both ways.

Your feelings and actions are, of course, also related. When you're happy (feeling), you might smile (behavior). And research shows that when you smile (behavior), the body releases neuropeptides along with dopamine, serotonin, and endorphins, which literally make us feel good (feeling).

Although thoughts, feelings, and behaviors are separate, distinct processes, they are all closely related. Having said that, thoughts are the fulcrum. In other words, your thoughts literally have the power to change everything.

So. Many. Thoughts.

Here's an important consideration when it comes to your thoughts: Without realizing it, thoughts are constantly swirling around your head. In fact, scientists estimate we have about 60,000 thoughts each day. Just imagine! That's 60,000 ideas, assumptions, attitudes, concerns, expectations, perceptions, interpretations, and beliefs—every single day!

What's more, for the average person, 50% or more of those thoughts are negative. Think about that. It's like looking at a football stadium where every seat is a thought, and over half are negative! Furthermore, the majority of those 60,000 thoughts you have today are the same darn thoughts you had yesterday—and the day before, and the day before.

For the most part, our thoughts are reflexive. In general, we do not consciously choose what we think. Our thoughts are, in a sense, on autopilot. And yet, thoughts are incredibly powerful! Thoughts are responsible for your happiness, the positive interactions you have, and your success in work and life. They're also often the cause of stress, strained relationships, and failure. That is how vital our thoughts are.

Why Thoughts Are So Darn Powerful

It's what you *say* to yourself about what's happening—not what's actually happening—that primarily impacts how you feel and what you do. From there, what you do and how you feel can further impact your thoughts and even reinforce them. This reciprocal relationship can then become a self-fulfilling prophecy. That is, what we think might happen often does happen.

Let's say you are going into a job interview for a position that you really want. It's more advanced than what you're doing now, so it's a bit of a stretch, but it really is your dream job.

Now, let's "try on" two different mindsets to see how changing your thoughts changes the outcome.

THOUGHT ONE: *Who am I kidding? This job is way out of my league. There's no way I'll get hired. I'm an idiot for agreeing to the interview.*

- *Event:* Interview

- *Feelings:* Anxious, nervous

- *Behaviors:* You avoid practicing your interview because it's so stressful. During the interview, you stumble over your words or have trouble concentrating on concise responses to the interview questions.

- *Consequence:* Interviewer declines to make you an offer

- *Internal Reaction:* "See? I'm completely inadequate."

THOUGHT TWO: *Yes, this job is a stretch. AND I'm ready for it!*

- *Event:* Interview

- *Feelings:* Excited, energized

- *Behaviors:* You do several mock interviews beforehand. During the interview, you are actively engaged, really listening to the interviewer, and providing concise responses.

- *Consequence:* Interviewer suggests you speak to two other people on her team.

- *Internal Reaction:* "Yay! I'm on my way to landing this job. And even if I don't, I know I left a positive impression, which can only be helpful in the future."

As you can see, thoughts can create a self-fulfilling prophecy. You may call it the Law of Attraction (where you attract the same energy that you are emitting), or it may simply be that how you think impacts how you interact with the world, which then impacts how the world interacts with you. It really doesn't matter which mechanism you believe in; what does matter is that you grasp how powerful your thoughts are so that you can take control of them.

What Are You Telling Yourself?

In order to control your thoughts, the first step is to determine what you are saying to yourself. As I often ask my coaching clients, "If you could stick a microphone in your mind, what would you hear yourself saying?"

Most of the time, we're not really aware of what we're thinking, but by becoming aware of the *consequences* of these thoughts, we can learn to change how we think. This takes some careful attention and can be surprising and even uncomfortable at first.

For example, Ellie was working with me on progressing in her corporate career. She had a terrific track record as a top sales executive and was highly respected by her peers. She had been with the company for two years and was ready to make a move up or out. However, she expressed fear and anxiety about asking her boss for a promotion. I asked her to identify her thoughts, feelings, and behavior in relation to the event to help her see the power of her thoughts. Here's what she expressed.

- *Event:* Opportunity for promotion
- *Thought:* What if he says no? What if he tells me I'm not good enough? I would be mortified.
- *Feelings:* Fear, anxiety
- *Behavior:* Avoiding speaking with my boss. Irritability with friends and family because of my frustration.

Immediately, Ellie saw how powerful her thoughts were. I asked her to put a new slide in the projector—one that feels true and is also positive. So she came up with a new thought: I owe it to myself to have this conversation with my boss and ask for what I want. I'm smart and accomplished and deserve to be heard.

This change in thought impacted Ellie's feelings and behavior—and she got the promotion!

Now it's your turn. Consider a recent event when you felt stressed. Or overwhelmed. Or anxious, scared, worried, angry, or any other feeling you didn't want. Identify the event, then write down your subsequent thoughts, feelings, and behaviors.

Can you see the power your thoughts have in driving your feelings and behaviors?

Now, you might be wondering, "Okay, Dr. E. So I get that my thoughts are powerful. Now what? How do I change them?"

We'll get to that—I promise!

What's vital to realize is that if we try to change your thoughts without fully understanding what you're saying to yourself, the change may not be helpful.

Let's say you took your car to a mechanic because it was making strange noises. The mechanic changed the belt because a faulty belt can result in strange noises. However, without really figuring out the exact cause of the sounds, changing the belt may or may not help with the situation.

You need to figure out the problem in order to find the best solution.

It's the same when it comes to your thoughts. You don't (necessarily) need to spend years in therapy uncovering every thought you have had since childhood. It is helpful, though, to really figure out what you're saying to yourself on a deeper level—to really "diagnose" your internal dialogue—so you can improve your mindset and, ultimately, your life.

So now you might be wondering, "With that many thoughts bumping around in my head all day, how can I know when one warrants further investigation?"

Great question. Yes, with the 60,000 thoughts racing daily through your mind, you won't be aware of all of them. But this is where we use the biofeedback we talked about earlier to notice when you're having a thought that might not be working for you. To do this: Whenever you have a feeling or behavior that you don't want, stop and ask, "What am I saying to myself?" Access that inner microphone!

The goal is to start using your feelings and behaviors as cues, like a "check engine" light that's reminding you to stop and take notice.

For example, when you notice a pit in your stomach (feeling), ask yourself, "What am I thinking right now?" Perhaps you're telling yourself you'll mess up, or that you can't handle the situation at hand.

If you notice worry, your inner voice may be shouting, "What if something terrible happens?" And when you react as if that negative outcome is imminent, you add even more distress.

Perhaps you notice a pattern of procrastination, like if you're putting off an important project. When you explore your thinking, you may realize you are saying, "I can't do it," or, "It will be a disaster, so why even bother?!"

The goal right now is to identify what you're saying to yourself that is causing your Red Flags.

Layers

Consider an onion. Or better yet, a croissant. When you peel off the outer layer, what do you have left? Another layer. Take that one off, and what's left? Yet another layer. You could go through multiple layers before you get to the core.

Similarly, certain thoughts or interpretations regarding what's going on can often be peeled back to reveal further layers of thought. So for example, if a neighbor plays music really loudly at night, you may notice yourself feeling angry. If I asked you why, you might say, "That music is keeping me awake." That outer layer of thinking is simple and straightforward.

Sometimes our thoughts stay at that outer layer, and sometimes they go deeper. It's the deeper thoughts that really contribute to how you feel, what you think, and what you do.

When feelings are strong (fury) and/or when resulting actions are severe (screaming at your neighbor to turn it down), it's likely there are some deeper thoughts going on.

For example, if you were in the Red Zone when the neighbor was playing loud music in the middle of the night, you might be aware of the concern that your sleep was being disrupted. On a deeper level, though, your thoughts might sound like, "My neighbor doesn't respect me. He doesn't think I'm worthy of having peace and quiet." And, as we will explore in the next chapter, when we get upset because we *think* someone is thinking about us in a negative way, it's actually because we may share at least part of that negative belief. So in this case, a Red Zone reaction to a neighbor playing loud music may be fueled by a deeper belief of, "I'm not worthy of respect." Ouch!

The goal is to identify the underlying and deeper level thoughts that are ultimately contributing to your feelings and behaviors.

How can you do this?

When you are exploring your thoughts, ask yourself the following questions to get a more comprehensive understanding of what you are saying to yourself:

- What does it mean to you?
- What is the worst part about it?
- Why would this be so bad?

- What does that say about the situation?
- What does that say about the other person/people?
- What does that say about you?

When Red Flags are present, that usually means we're personalizing external events or viewing circumstances in an overly negative manner.

So for my client above, Ellie, who was fearful about asking for the promotion, her obvious automatic thoughts that were causing her distress and avoidance were, "What if they say no? I'll feel like a complete failure at this."

And that is a pretty tough belief. The distress and Red Flags signaled that more was going on than feeling like a failure at work.

So I asked her some thought-provoking questions to peel back the layers:

Me: What does it mean to you if they say no?
Ellie: It means I'm in the wrong career.

Me: If that were true, what's the worst part about it?
Ellie: That I made the wrong decision in taking this job. That I, once again, am failing at what I want to do. I'm an embarrassment to my husband and family.

Me: If that were true, what does that say about you?
Ellie: That I should stop now before I waste more time and energy. I'm a failure at everything I do. I'm worthless.

That is deep.

So she went from fear of rejection to feeling worthless and like a complete failure at *everything*. And those deep-seated beliefs caused her to procrastinate, making her avoid the conversation with her boss. It also prevented her from being assertive and welcoming feedback if the decision on the promotion was a "no."

The mitigating thoughts were not reflecting reality. They were, however, determining reality.

Our thoughts are powerful, even if we're not always aware of their existence. The key is to be more aware, and ultimately change the ones that aren't working for you. We'll explore more about how to do the latter in future sections.

In doing so, we'll look at specific thinking patterns the brain tends to use when experiencing high levels of distress. And in a later chapter, we'll explore how to control your stress so that it doesn't control you. For now, be aware of how intense distress can impact your thinking.

To do that, identify a time in the past few weeks when you were in the Red Zone. Consider what happened (the event), what feelings you had and how intense they were (on a scale from zero to ten), and what you did. Then, identify the different layers of your thoughts that were fueling your distress.

To dig deeper into your thoughts, consider the following.

- For each feeling you listed above, *why* did you feel like that?

- For each behavior, *why* did you act like that?
- Why did you not do something different?
- If the thoughts you identified were, in fact, true, what does that say about you, the situation, and those involved?
- What would be the worst part if these thoughts were true?

Can you see the power of distress on your thoughts?

Clear-Headed View of Thoughts

Sometimes, identifying your thoughts when you're stressed out can be tricky. Remember, when we're experiencing distress, our limbic system overrides our rational thinking. So when we resume more moderate levels of stress, our rational thinking comes back online. It can be difficult for a more rational brain to recall the thinking that took place when we were in limbic-system-hijack mode.

I worked with a highly successful single mom named Amy. Amy's son recently got into trouble at school. When the school's principal called her about it, she slipped into the Red Zone. She even acted out, yelling and behaving in ways that were out of character for her, so she reached out to me for help. Amy reported that her distress level had been at a nine out of ten when the principal called. She felt anger, frustration, and help-lessness. The day we talked, however, her distress level had subsided. She described it as three out of ten.

When I asked what thoughts Amy's internal micro-phone picked up in her brain, she was able to identify the thought, "He doesn't listen to me." I then asked her what that meant about her as a mother, or what it means about any mother when their child defies them. Amy thought for a while and then said, "It must mean I'm a bad parent, but I don't really believe that about myself."

Certainly, I am glad Amy doesn't see herself as a bad mother. At the same time, given her high level of distress, I knew there was something deeper within her thinking, something that was a more global and impactful belief. Otherwise, she would have felt less distress.

To assist Amy, I asked that she try to think with her nine out of ten distressed mind, rather than her three out of ten distressed mind. I reminded her that at higher levels of distress, human thinking is hijacked by the limbic system—it's emotional and not rational. I asked her to imagine what she was thinking when she was in the Red Zone. Amy closed her eyes. She was able to recall that during the event, she thought she was a bad parent, and she believed that this one transgression would lead to an onslaught of inevitable doom for her son, herself, and her family. Right away, she recognized that in the Red Zone, her thinking had been skewed. Her emotions and behaviors were impacted by those thoughts.

It's pretty remarkable that we humans have the ability to recall thoughts experienced during times of distress. Once we have resumed lower levels of stress, we have the chance to make corrections. What a gift! So as you're going through this exercise, accept this gift and really challenge yourself to recall your thinking when you were in the Red Zone. The information you glean will likely be quite eye-opening.

No Judgment Here

As you attempt to identify thoughts you had during Red Zone events, resist the urge to judge yourself. All these thoughts are racing around your head, whether you acknowledge them or not. Taking control of your thoughts, rather than letting them control you, is key. It's vital that you acknowledge them as a first step.

Imagine you've injured your knee, and it just isn't healing as quickly as you'd like. If you went to a doctor, they might recommend an MRI to see what was going on. Let's say the MRI revealed a torn ACL. Would you judge that ACL for being ruptured? I doubt it. Having the information that the pain is being caused by a torn ACL illuminates a path to healing and health.

Consider this exercise a sort of Thought MRI, allowing you to pinpoint thoughts contributing to your emotional pain and counterproductive behaviors.

Dropping an imaginary microphone into your brain to discover your thoughts in the Red Zone illustrates a profound truth: A stressed-out brain is rarely a rational one. In the next chapter, we will explore *why* we experience distorted thinking—and how to change that pattern.

Chapter Five

Seeing Clearly in the Red Zone: Spotting Cognitive Distortions

When I was little, I loved to try on my father's ginormous tortoise shell rimmed glasses. They were a bit oversized, even for him—this was the 70s, after all—and on me, they were huge. Additionally, my dad had worn glasses for over three decades by that point, and his prescription was pretty strong. He joked that his lenses were made from old Coca-Cola bottles. When I put those big glasses on my tiny noggin, everything around me suddenly seemed blurry. I could make out vague forms in front of me, but if I tried to walk around with them on, I inevitably bumped into something. They made my depth perception terrible. When I removed those glasses, the world came back into sharp focus again as my 20/20 vision returned. I could get back to climbing trees, Legos, and playing with my stuffed animals.

As an adult, I'm careful to avoid wearing anyone else's prescription glasses. It's no fun to see things in a distorted and blurry fashion. Plus, I prefer not to bump into things any more than I already do! So when I started to hold menus in nicer restaurants at arm's length just to make out the text, I didn't just pick up a random pair of glasses. I consulted an optometrist and got the right pair for me. Now, I wear my glasses with the right lenses, and I'm seeing things clearly, even in dimly lit restaurants. Turns out the right lenses make all the difference.

When it comes to thinking clearly, none of us have the equivalent of 20/20 vision. Humans are simply not capable of being perfectly rational 100% of the time. It doesn't matter how smart you are, how old you are, or what your IQ is. Especially in the Red Zone, the limbic hijack tends to skew our thinking. What's worse, this can happen *without us even realizing it.*

Stinkin' Thinkin'

Fortunately, psychologists have identified common patterns of irrational thinking. Once we identify them, we can compensate for those errors, much like a prescriptive lens compensates for less-than-perfect vision. The clinical term for such patterns is cognitive distortions. *Cognitive* refers to thinking, and *distortion* describes your thinking as inaccurate, errored, or even blatantly false. Cognitive distortions reinforce negative feelings or beliefs. A less clinical term is "stinkin' thinkin'."

I've found that helping my corporate clients spot cognitive distortions is key to achieving True Success™. So in this chapter, we will explore cognitive distortions so you, too, can determine the role these tricky buggers play in your thoughts. If you're (1) human, and (2) honest with yourself, you'll see some that apply to your personal and professional life. (I know I do!) The goal? I want you to learn to easily spot distorted thinking, even when your distress levels escalate.

This Is Normal

Remember that cognitive distortions are *completely* normal. Every human experiences them from time to time. Wearing the wrong prescription glasses isn't harmful unless you don't know you're wearing them, because you don't know to take them off. Similarly, cognitive distortions only impair you if you're ignorant of them. Again, becoming aware of your thoughts, right or wrong, allows you to control them, instead of letting them control you.

Below is a list of common cognitive distortions. We will explore the impact of each in the subsequent sections:

- Negative filtering
- All-or-nothing
- Blaming
- Fortune-telling
- Over generalizing
- Regret orientation
- Mind reading
- Should-ing

I call these distortions NAB FORMS as an acronym to remember them. These forms of thinking will nab your rational thinking.

Negative Filtering

Negative filtering is a pattern of focusing on what is wrong to the exclusion of seeing what is right. This thinking pattern is especially prevalent when we're in the Red Zone. Absorbing only negative information leads to increased feelings of distress.

For example, Joy was a single mom with four children under the age of 12. She came to see me, exhausted, and shared, "I worked 60+ hours a week. When I got home, I wanted to enjoy my family, but could I? No! All they do is take and take and don't appreciate me at all."

As we talked more, it became apparent that Joy's two oldest often thanked her for dinner, grocery shopping, and even driving the carpool. And yet when she was in the Red Zone, she couldn't see their appreciation.

Now, evolutionarily, there is a good reason for negative filtering. I mean, back in caveman times, if our ancestors heard a noise and thought, "I'm going to ignore that. It's probably nothing," they may have gotten consumed by one of their predators. Negative filtering may have been quite helpful back then when a sound could mean imminent danger. It's important to remember, though, that stress during prehistoric times was more event-related (when a predator was near). After the event was over, there was no more distress. That's in sharp contrast to modern life when stress is an everyday—sometimes every minute—experience.

All-or-Nothing

All-or-nothing cognitive distortions classify using two categories with no middle ground. We see this commonly with those who have a perfectionist mindset:

One mistake = Complete failure.

Every year, millions of Americans make unreasonable all-or-nothing promises to themselves on January 1st. We say things like, "I'm giving up all sugar and booze, and I'm going to exercise every day." Then January 17th comes along (which is apparently "National Quitter's Day"), and those all-or-nothing pledges get dropped by the wayside. "I had one cookie and ruined my diet, might as well eat the rest of the plate." Or, "I can't get to the gym this week because I'm so busy; I guess I just won't be able to work out."

All or nothing. Perfection or failure. Perfect or forget it.

I'm intimately acquainted with this cognitive distortion. I spent decades in its grip before I figured out how to deal. I even wrote an entire book about it! *Better Than Perfect: 7 Strategies to Crush Your Inner Critic and Create a Life You Love.*

Blaming

When a person places 100% of responsibility on their circumstances and fails to own any responsibility, that's blaming.

I see this a lot with people who take on the role of a victim. They're stuck in their misery because they view their current situation as being completely caused by someone else. Now don't get me wrong. Having worked with clients for over two decades, I can tell you that I have heard some horrible stories regarding events like child abuse, domestic abuse, physical abuse, emotional abuse, conniving, stealing, affairs, etc., and it's absolutely vital that people work through even the most horrific events so that they can move forward.

Now, please hear me say this from a place of love and empowerment: What happened in the past, happened in the past. Your reaction right now is a direct result of what's going on in your mind, or what you are saying to yourself. While we can't change the past, we can change how you react to what happened in the past. We can also change what you're doing now.

Consider Scott, whose wife of 22 years had an affair. Needless to say, this was an excruciating discovery for Scott. When he first came to see me, over two years had passed. He was still palpably bitter. He described tense relationships with his children and serious issues at work. "I blame her. This is all Debbie's fault." Scott blamed Debbie for everything that was going wrong in his life, which prevented him from ever being *able* to take action or create change. He was perpetually stuck in the Red Zone, and had given someone else the key to unlock the door.

Getting out of the Red Zone is not about whose fault the past experience was; it's about what *you* can do now.

Even though the situation may not be caused by you, you *can* do something about it.

Fortune-Telling

I once did a segment on the Dr. Oz Show on "toxic worry." We asked the audience if any of them worry and, if so about what. Without exception, every person there admitted to worry, citing such topics as job security, their children's education, and their health.

Worry is "what-if" thinking. For example, "What if I mess up my presentation? What if my child gets sick?

What if the client rejects our offer?" Used positively, what-if thinking can be productive, providing an imaginative pathway to great things! But worry? This type of what-if thinking conjectures that something negative is about to happen, then the person reacts emotionally as if that negative outcome is imminent.

Worry is a type of fortune-telling, because you are predicting the future negatively and reacting as if what you fear is impending, or a certainty.

How do we know this is happening in our thinking? Because of the consequences of our thoughts.

With fortune-telling, the thought, "What if I mess up my presentation?" is quickly followed by, "I will get fired," or something else unpleasant. We know this to be true because of the resulting feelings of anxiety and fear. If this wasn't the case, if the only thought was, "What if I mess up my presentation?" without the predicted answer, then, instead of worry, you'd simply experience curiosity or wonder.

Fortune-telling is like putting your winter coat on in the summer. Imagine that it's a gorgeous summer day. You're meeting a friend for lunch in an outdoor café when your friend walks up wearing a long winter coat, scarf, and hat. Wouldn't you think something was a little strange? When you ask your friend about his strange costume, he replies that winter is just four months away. That still makes no sense, right? Sweating for four months until it's cold is *unnecessary* discomfort. And yet that's what we do when we predict the future negatively—we emotionally react as if something negative is already happening or inevitable, even when that's not accurate or true.

Overgeneralizing

In overgeneralizing, a broad negative assumption is made based on limited knowledge or information.

Jody was upset about how her colleague treated her. "She just joined a few weeks ago, and she's always so rude." When asked for evidence of this assumption, Jody said, "Last week, during a team meeting, I was giving a presentation when she proceeded to question what I was saying." In Jody's mind, this one-time action indicated that the colleague was "against" her. Jody's hyperfocus on that one interaction blinded her to the big picture: This may very well have been a colleague eager to learn about her new company and work with her team to make things even better.

In overgeneralizing, Jody was wearing a pair of glasses that distorted her vision. Certain words signal the use of overgeneralizing. Examples include:

- Always
- Never
- No one
- Every
- All the time
- Forever

Regret Orientation

Thus far, we've been thinking of cognitive distortions as prescriptive lenses that distort rather than enhance vision. Regret orientation, however, is more like driving a car using only the rear-view mirror. It's a pattern of thinking focused on the past instead of present and future possibilities.

Regret orientation often sounds like "if only."

Consider Collin, who invested a significant amount of money in the stock market. When he lost over half of his savings, he was devastated, scared, and extremely embarrassed. He became stuck in thinking, "If only I hadn't invested all that money, then I wouldn't be stressed, then I could sleep at night, then I could actually retire before the age of 80." He fixated on what happened in the past and felt like a victim to his actions.

This kind of thinking is tricky because it feels honest, but it's not.

One of the issues with regret orientation is that it keeps you stuck in the past because of the belief that things today would only be better if something different had happened previously. It reminds me of a math equation.

If you have completed a simple computation: $1 + 2 = 3$

Then you would also be able to say: $3 = 1 + 2$

Your mind would register that each side has the same value. The equal sign, of course, means what is on one side is equivalent to the other.

This is how that equation translates to regret orientation:

> *If only* X had not happened = Things would be okay (I could forgive her, I could be happy, I could move forward, etc.).

Unfortunately, in addition to this, our mind also hears:

> Things would be okay (I could forgive her, I could be happy, I could move forward, etc.) = *If only* X had not happened.

In essence, what we are saying is: I could only forgive, be happy, move forward (or any other positive experience) IF and ONLY if something that has already happened was different.

And that, of course, is impossible. We cannot go back in time (at least, not as of the date I am writing this book). As a result, this type of thinking really sets us up for failure. When using regret orientation, the inability to change the past means we cannot successfully live in the present or move forward into the future.

The way to deal with regret orientation is to focus on what you can do.

Mind Reading

Logic dictates that we cannot *actually* know what's going on in another person's mind. Yet with mind reading, we presume others are having negative thoughts about us. For example, we might think:

- My boss gave me this assignment just to test me.
- She doesn't like me.
- They must think I'm stupid.

When we trick ourselves into thinking we know others' thoughts, we often act as if our assumption is fact. This creates a self-fulfilling prophecy. Think about it: If you believe that Joe thinks you're a complete loser, how are you going to interact with him? Maybe you'll feel nervous, or bitter, or resentful, or shy. And how would that impact your interactions with Joe? You might avoid him. You might act strangely around him. You might be rude or passive-aggressive toward him. The result could be a self-fulfilling prophecy where, because of your interactions, Joe really does start to think less-than-highly of you.

A second issue of mind reading is that if someone thinks negatively about you, it only hurts if it's your own fear. Eleanor Roosevelt famously said, "No one can make you feel inferior without your consent." That means you have to at least partially agree with what the other person is saying—or in this case, thinking—in order for it to hurt. Think about it.

For example, are you confident in your ability to walk? Maybe not in high heels or after a few glasses of wine, but are you confident in your ability to walk in general? Most readers would say, "Sure, I'm a capable walker." Now, what if someone said, "You're a really bad walker." Would that upset you? Would that make you cry or feel like a failure? Probably not. In fact, you probably wouldn't be hurt by that at all. You might wonder why they said that, but it probably wouldn't hurt your feelings.

So when you find yourself mind reading, it's a great opportunity to identify the thought you're attributing to someone else, then consider the possibility that you're falsely attributing a thought to them. If so see it as an opportunity to take steps to address it—to change the slide.

Should-ing

When we use the word "should" when assessing ourselves, others, or a situation, it can signal that we're falling into the trap of "should-ing." The word "should" is based on judging; judging how you think things *should* be, rather than how they are.

When we "should" ourselves, we feel guilt and shame.

When we "should" others, we often feel angry and resentful.

When we "should" ourselves and/or others, it is an indication that our "rules" have been broken. You see, we all have certain rules about how we believe people *should* act, think, and be. Oftentimes, we're not aware of the rules, per se, until they are broken. And when they are broken, that is when we often zoom into the Red Zone.

Consider Lisa, who was feeling extremely overwhelmed. She had a big project due on Thursday, and by Monday, she was feeling resentful toward her colleagues. "They should be helping out," she told me.

When I asked her why she thought that, she responded, "Because we're all part of a team." You see, Lisa's rule was that a team should voluntarily support each other. She hadn't openly asked because, according to her rules, if they wanted to help, they would. Or really, if they wanted to help, they *should* volunteer. And because no one was jumping in to assist, she felt angry and resentful.

I also see a lot of should-ing when it comes to couples. This thinking sounds like, "My partner *should* be more supportive," or, "My partner *should* be grateful for all of the work that I do." That kind of thinking results in feelings of anger and resentment. It also tends to strain relationships and increase distress for all parties involved.

The Right Rx Advantage

Do any of these cognitive distortions sound familiar? I thought so.

Now, before you start being critical of yourself, please realize these distortions are common—in fact, very common. Rarely do people stop and ask, "How accurate and helpful is my thinking right now?" Most people seldom, if ever, do.

You, however, are not striving to be "ordinary," are you? The fact that you're reading this book tells me that you're aiming for much more. This book is for those who want an extraordinary life.

Now that you know about these distortions, you have an edge. Understanding that you use distortions from time to time sets you apart. Yes, those thoughts scrambling through your mind are impacting you. By even questioning the validity of the thought, you are in a position of power.

"Where Did These Numbers Come From?"

Imagine you are the CFO of a huge company. As you plan for your next fiscal year, you pore over the profit and loss statements from your company's previous year.

Using that information, you make predictions for the following year.

But what if those P&L statements are faulty, inaccurate, or even fabricated? How accurate will your financial forecast be? Not very. And, as a result, you will probably not be a very successful CFO (or even still employed).

That's what happens with unrecognized cognitive distortions. We base judgments and decisions on erroneous information. And to make matters worse, we are often completely unaware we are doing it. But what happens if, as CFO, you call out the fact that the numbers aren't adding up? You question the numbers and dig in. Then you have an advantage, because you're ready to make empowered, accurate decisions.

Similarly, becoming aware of your own biased thinking will help you take control of your thoughts, resulting in more positive feelings and actions. This can translate into more success in your business, more fulfilling relationships, greater self-confidence, and a whole host of other benefits.

Cognitive Distortions in the Red Zone

When we are in the Red Zone, we're more likely to unconsciously use distorted thinking because of that limbic system hijack that goes on, and that distorted thinking can cause even more problems and distress. To stop that cycle, let's look at how distortions play a role in your life, because one of the first steps to changing your thoughts is to realize when the ones you are having are not 100% accurate or helpful.

To help you do that, try the following exercise:

Identify a time in the past few weeks when you were in the Red Zone. List:

- The event (what happened);
- Your feelings;
- Your thoughts (what your internal microphone picked up); and
- Any cognitive distortions you may have been using.

Later, we will discover how to overcome these distortions. For now, though, it's important to practice raising your awareness to when you are using them.

Chapter Six

Thought Pathways:
Traversing the Landscape of Your Brain

When we're in the Red Zone, inundated with stress, our bodies go into "conserve energy" mode. We take the path of least resistance to conserve energy—which is helpful when you're a caveman trying to escape a predator. But the path of least resistance isn't always in our best interest in the long run—humans have very few predators these days.

So if our thoughts are sending us into the Red Zone, the question becomes, "How do we change our thoughts?"

Let's take a closer look at thoughts.

Open-Field Thinking

Imagine thoughts as pathways. Each thought is a result of certain nerves firing in the brain, traversing across neuron pathways like tiny bursts of energy traveling across the expanse of your brain. Figuratively speaking, such paths get worn smooth with wear. The second time across is easier than the first, and the third time is easier still.

When I was a kid, we used to visit friends who lived in a very rural area. We called them our "country cousins." They had a farm with chickens (the nicest one was named after my mother) and a big garden with peacocks that sauntered around from time to time. They also had acres and acres of overgrown fields. I'm actually not sure why they lived on a farm, because they didn't really *use* their property as a functioning farm, but it was a lot of fun as a child. We used to run around for hours, playing hide and seek (I loved hiding in the loft of the barn), cops and robbers, and other games we made up on the fly.

Sometimes the fields were so overgrown with vegetation that, if you ran into the field and sat down, you could almost be hidden. And the cool part was, when you walked through the fields, you could create a pathway that left the grass trampled down so that the next time you wanted to walk that way, there was a more established pathway.

As you can imagine, the more frequently we took a specific path, the more the grass got pushed down, and eventually, the grass was gone, replaced by a dirt path. That well-trodden dirt path became the path of least resistance when it came to traversing the field.

Our thinking is very much like this field. Once we've created a thought pathway, we're more likely to have that thought again and again. The more frequently a thought occurs, the stronger the connection grows and the more automatic that thought becomes. I refer to this process as Open-Field Thinking (OFT), which I first introduced in *Better Than Perfect*.

Wiring Thoughts Together

Consider the ABC song. If you grew up in the United States, you probably learned the alphabet set to Mozart. And while you may not have sung this melody in a while, as soon as someone sings the first three letters—"A, B, C"—to you, the tune immediately comes to mind. Why? Because that song has basically been imprinted into your brain. The nerves have fired together so many times that they are "wired" together. Those thoughts (or lyrics) have become automatic.

Now, what if you were asked to recite your ABC's without singing the childhood tune? That might be difficult, because that is asking your brain to go down a new path. In fact, while it's not endorsed by the National Highway Traffic Safety Administration (NHTSA) as a sobriety test, some police officers suspecting an incidence of driving under the influence request that the driver recite a portion of the alphabet *without* singing. This can be a challenge for a taxed brain because it requires extra brain power. Remember, when we're under stress, our bodies seek the most efficient paths—even though these might not be beneficial in the long run.

These deeply grooved paths become our beliefs. They become assumptions, biases, and "rules" for life that may or may not be accurate. Our beliefs—true or not—then influence our thoughts, feelings, and behaviors, as we've already discovered.

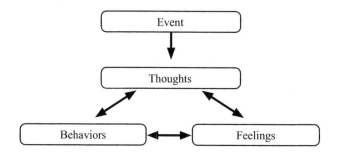

How Faulty Beliefs Develop

Let's say you grew up in a stressful household. Maybe the adults in your home were dealing with their own issues, so teaching unconditional love was not something they even knew how to do. When you did something wrong, you got in trouble. When you stayed quiet or out of trouble, there was greater peace. And greater peace was what you longed for.

If this was the case (as it was for many of my clients), you may have grown up with the idea: "I have to be 'good' in order for people to like me." From that, a need to be a people-pleaser possibly grew. You developed the belief that, "I am only loveable if I make people happy." As a result, when people around you were upset, you personalized that to mean you messed up, and, on a deeper level, that you failed and are not worthy of love, or peace.

This belief would then impact how you interpret specific events. If, for example, you have the belief that, "I am only loveable if I make people happy," then when a partner, colleague, or child gets upset with you, you're likely to interpret that discontent as indicative that you're not loveable—especially when you're in the Red Zone. This then reinforces the path you've already created.

Inadequate Affirmations

Another reinforcing behavior is often the inadvertent result of an attempt to change our brain pathways. Have you ever tried daily affirmations? Affirmations are positive (affirming) statements like:

- I'm going to meet the love of my life.
- I will earn a million dollars.

Affirmations can be helpful if the statements we tell ourselves are truthful. But if you don't believe any part of the affirmation, deep down, you'll reject it. It would be as if you're declaring, "I can fly like a bird." You know this to be impossible, so you won't form a new path. The reason behind this is because statements which contradict your beliefs are often rejected as false.

When true, however, these helpful statements push down the grass, so to speak, toward making positive thought pathways clearer and more efficient, which our brain prefers.

So how can we start to change our beliefs so they work for and not against us? This is the subject of our next chapter.

Chapter Seven

Your Super-Efficient Brain: Conscious & Unconscious Thinking

Once upon a time, there was a legendary CEO. It was rumored that the key to his success was his magical, invisible executive assistant. The CEO's phone calls, hundreds of pieces of incoming mail, and packages were all received and triaged by the assistant with incredible speed. The assistant tagged and efficiently delivered only the most vital communications to the CEO. Everything else, the assistant filed away in the archives, freeing the CEO up to focus solely on critical decisions and planning. With the help of this magical assistant, the CEO led the company into its most successful period in history.

Would you like to have such a helpful assistant? Good news! You have one, and it's called your subconscious. The CEO in this scenario? Your conscious mind.

Like any CEO's office, the human brain is bombarded by incoming information. Multiply the amount of incoming information by several million to get an accurate picture of what the brain takes in, because it's *billions* of pieces of information coming in at any given *second*. (Yes, you read that right: billions!) Making sense of all this incoming data is a staggering challenge.

The subconscious mind is your magical assistant doing all the behind-the-scenes information sorting. It works so quickly and efficiently that it is, in effect, on autopilot. Habits, core beliefs, fight-or-flight reactions, and involuntary bodily functions reside here. Around 90% of brain processing happens at this level. To simplify this idea, consider your subconscious as the part of the iceberg that is below the surface—though it's invisible to the naked eye, it's an impactful reality.

The conscious mind is analytical, rational, and problem solving. Conscious thought processing is that which we're aware of. The conscious brain has a limited capacity. Liken it to the tip of the iceberg—the part above the water that's visible. Scientists tell us that only about 10% of brain function is conscious.

Huge Processing Disparity

While the CEO calls the shots, the executive assistant is undeniably powerful. Think about it: The conscious brain processes about 40 bits of information in any given moment while the subconscious processes about *two million* bits of information. It would be like one person reading a chapter of a book while another speed-reads an entire library!

To conserve energy and deal with the "workload" of all the incoming data, the subconscious develops certain shortcuts. It constantly interprets the environment and makes decisions on how to react based on existing beliefs, assumptions, and biases. Going back to our grassy field analogy, why create new paths if there's a well-worn path already, right? So the subconscious interprets events and even makes "rules" to help process information more quickly.

The conscious mind chooses which path it wants to take. The subconscious mind involuntarily takes the path of least resistance. A thought can be represented by a path with its grass newly trampled down. A belief, or a deep-seated thought, is a well-worn pathway deeply etched in the field of the subconscious mind.

Creating New Thoughts

Suppose you have a new thought or idea. You're taking an uncharted route through a grassy field. Trampling down the high grass is good, but it's not as efficient as taking a more well-traveled path. It takes more time and effort. The next time you have a choice: Take the route with the grass pushed down by your recent walk, or take the path worn down to bare dirt from constant use. The latter offers the least resistance, making it the easiest choice—especially if you're in a hurry and resources are scarce. When this choice is left to your subconscious, you're more likely to take that old path.

Let's say a deep-seated belief about yourself is, "I am bad at math." You probably take that path hundreds of times each day, subconsciously. So even if you consciously assert, "I'm good at math" ten times each day, which thought is likely to offer the least resistance: the one taken ten times or hundreds of times each day?

The great disparity between the conscious and subconscious minds explains why a new thought (like saying, "I believe in myself") alone won't get you out of the Red Zone. Although you're saying one thing, on a deeper level, your subconscious refutes it and goes with the most efficient route.

What gets me excited is the knowledge that it's absolutely possible to change our thoughts in other ways. I'm about to share what I know about this with you!

But first, here are some reasons the subconscious may reject a new thought.

Cognitive Biases

As we're deluged with mass amounts of information at any given moment, it's a challenge to sort through it all. Cognitive biases determine which information gets the attention of the conscious mind. Even the most efficient—and magical—assistant uses shortcuts and filing systems to aid in the sorting process. Cognitive biases can be attributed to the need for efficiency or energy conservation. We use them to aid in the making of quick decisions by giving priority to some information over others. Even though biases can help streamline things, sometimes these "shortcuts" hinder more than they help. Two main cognitive biases are: The Bandwagon Effect and Choice-Supportive Bias.

The Bandwagon Effect is the tendency to do what the majority of people do or think without rationally considering all the options. I recently witnessed this bias at play in an airport. Passing by a food court in search of some food, I saw that there were dozens of people in line at the various restaurants. I had plenty of time before my flight, so I hopped in line at the sandwich place. Twenty minutes later, I walked away with my food, only to discover that there was another place to get the same sandwich I had just waited for less than twenty yards away, and it had very few patrons. The lines in the food court indicated to me that many people had already made the choice, so like many others, I didn't even evaluate other choices that might be available. I simply joined in.

Choice-Supportive Bias gives positive preference to choices already made, even if evidence contradicts the initial decision. That is, once you've made a choice about something, you only acknowledge that which supports your decision, and dismiss any evidence to the contrary. Ever wonder why it's so darn hard to get rid of clothes you've bought but haven't worn in years? That's simply Choice-Support Bias playing a role. You decided to buy those articles of clothing, so your subconscious ignores evidence of any less than stellar apparel choices.

I see this play out with corporate clients in myriad ways. For example, Allen recruited Desmond to his team. Desmond struggled to adapt to the job, leaving the rest of the team overworked as they picked up his slack. Yet Allen continued to champion Desmond. When team members asked about Desmond, Allen justified his hiring decision, saying, "It's just taking longer than usual for Desmond to figure things out. Let's give him another few months," rather than making necessary changes for the good of the team, based on the evidence.

Once a decision is made, Choice-Support Bias makes evaluating new information difficult. It's like tunnel vision, and it's especially strong in the Red Zone.

Learned Helplessness

Another potential influence on our subconscious is learned helplessness, which refers to the belief that there is nothing we can do to change uncomfortable circumstances.

I call this the "Cable Guy Syndrome." My family and I moved a few times before our daughters entered elementary school. Each time we moved, I would call the cable company to come set up our cable and internet. There would be a time slot, say between 9am and noon, when the technician was scheduled to arrive. Inevitably, it would be 11:00am, 12:30pm, 1:15pm, and the cable guy wouldn't show up. Feeling as though I had no control over when the technician would actually arrive, inevitably left me in a space of learned helplessness. Subsequently, the perceived lack of control I had over the situation would propel me into the Red Zone.

Maybe you can relate? Perhaps you've experienced something similar when it comes to a colleague or family member. The COVID-19 pandemic, with its many forced regulations and rules (including time spent in quarantine), became a source of learned helplessness for many people.

Emotion-Focused Coping

Cognitive biases can cloud clear thinking, yet they demonstrate a positive truth: Our brains are wired for efficiency. We often make choices based on what seems like the "easiest" solution. Wisdom and experience teaches that easy isn't always best—in fact, when it comes to thinking clearly, there are always at least two strategies available to cope when we feel stuck:

- Problem-focused coping
- Emotion-focused coping

With *problem-focused coping*, we work to tangibly improve a problematic situation; that is, we change what is happening. With *emotion-focused coping*, we work instead to improve our emotional reactions to a problematic situation.

Energy spent on problem-focused approaches can certainly be helpful, but sometimes we can't change the situation because it is simply out of our control. Other times, thinking straight is difficult because the situation itself is so overwhelming. Addressing the emotional reaction is *always* something we can control, so with my clients and in my own life, I find it beneficial to address the emotional reaction first and foremost. Not only does it *feel* better, but it also gets you out of the Red Zone, allowing you to rationally address the situation.

Chapter Eight

"Now What, Dr. E?"

Now that we have explored the Red Zone, why people get into the Red Zone, the pivotal role thoughts and beliefs play when it comes to reacting in the Red Zone, and how the mind works, you might be thinking, "There is a lot going on in my mind! I'm not sure I can change it! Am I doomed?"

Look, you didn't come out of your mother's womb thinking thoughts like, "I can't do that," or, "I'm a failure." All thoughts are *learned*. And anything learned can be unlearned and relearned.

Healthy Thinking at Any Age

When I was a psychology student in my late 20s, I looked more like I was a teenager. This sometimes caused issues with new clients.

During my training, I worked in the field of psycho-oncology helping people diagnosed with cancer deal with the psychological pressures they were experiencing. As a student, I would work with clients using a specific protocol my supervisor and mentor had created. It was a problem-solving therapy approach to dealing with whatever struggles someone might be facing.

As you can imagine, there was a heightened level of distress for a lot of my clients, which made sense. They were dealing with significant health issues, and they were feeling so overwhelmed that they sought out psychological support.

Tara was a 67-year-old woman receiving medical treatment for ovarian cancer. She was depressed, fearful, angry (her abdominal pain that had been a symptom of the cancer had been dismissed by her primary care physician for over a year), and very concerned about dying. During our first session, as soon as I closed the therapy room door, she abruptly asked, "How old are you? How can you possibly help me?"

Luckily, I was able to convince her to just try working together for a few sessions before she made a decision to stop working with me. With a suspicious look, she agreed, then said, "I've been feeling depressed for years. I don't know how you can change that."

Fortunately, I did not have to change her; she changed herself. Within three sessions, she was feeling better emotionally. "I thought you were too young," she said. "I guess I thought wrong."

How was Tara able to change herself, despite feeling depressed for years? She learned a new way of thinking.

Uncrossing the Wires

My grandmother was a psychiatric nurse by training. She was also an incredible piano player. In her spare time, she liked to teach people the piano. She called her method, "How to play the piano despite years of practice."

That always got a laugh! How to play the piano *despite* years of practice. She worked with her students to identify the skills they'd been using that were not helpful—for instance, holding their wrists in an unideal position. In short, she helped them get rid of habits that interfered with successful piano playing.

At the same time, she taught them new skills that were effective. Her students learned to play *without* using the old, unhelpful skills, and instead using new, effective ones. The result? Their piano playing skills all improved—and they felt greater joy.

Think about it: By getting rid of what doesn't work, learning what does work, and practicing those skills, you'll improve dramatically.

That's what we're doing together.

Even if you have been experiencing the limbic hijack of the Red Zone with all its subsequent thoughts, feelings, and behaviors for as long as you can remember, you can retrain your brain. Even if you are going through a really challenging time—or are still feeling the impact of a challenge from the past—this book can help you. How do I know? Because I have worked with thousands of people in coaching and training sessions and seen the positive results.

In the remainder of this book, we will explore strategies to help you get out of—and stay out of—the Red Zone.

Let's go!

Chapter Nine

Transform Stress and Optimize True Success™

Have you ever fantasized about running away from it all and living on the beach? No spouse, no kids, no job, just a drink in your hand and the ocean waves…

Most of us have had this dream a time or two.

People often think of stress as bad. However, the notion of "getting rid of your stress" is not only impossible, but also counterproductive. In truth, stress is essential.

Lab Rats

In the early 1900's, two psychologists were looking at how to motivate lab mice to scurry through a maze. To get them moving, they provided some external motivation (an electric shock). Turns out, a moderate amount of stimulus (i.e.: the electrifying shock) prompted the mice to go through the maze. Too much of a jolt, though, and the mice scattered around in a disorganized and fearful attempt to escape. Too little, and they weren't motivated to move at all.

In psychology, this principle is called the Yerkes-Dodson Law, named after these two psychologists who were playing with the rodents. Specifically, the law states: "Increased physical or psychological arousal increases performance to a certain point and then diminishes performance with the intensity passed that point." Or, what I call the "Goldilocks Principle"—not too much and not too little.

What does this classic experiment have to do with your life and business?

While you may sometimes feel like you are in a rat race, the message here is the importance of optimizing your stress.

Eustress v. Distress

Sitting on a barstool in a chilly room with my hair coiffed and my make-up done, the camera guy counts down, "Five, four, three..." His hand signals: "Two, one," and he points at us. We're live via satellite in the homes of millions of viewers around the country. It's a segment on *The Today Show* focusing on stress. Hoda Kotb throws out a question. "Some stress can be a good thing, right?" My response? "Absolutely!"

The behind-the-scenes story is that I was in the middle of quite a bit of stress at that point in my life, and the rush of that stress was invigorating me at that very moment—filling me with energy and enthusiasm. My stress was optimized, and I was using it to my benefit.

Here's the deal. When we talk about stress, it's important to understand two key factors:

1. The intensity and
2. The type of stress.

When we talk about the Red Zone, we're mostly thinking of distress, which refers to the not-so-pleasant feelings associated with stress.

However, distress has a more positive counterpart: eustress. Eustress can include feelings such as passion, enthusiasm, excitement, elation, adventure, animation... eustress is what someone might experience when they are getting married, planning for vacation, or anticipating a positive project or event.

Let's consider how to use your stress to help motivate you. Eustress, in the form of excitement, can motivate you to push through challenges. Just like the rats in the experiment, a certain amount can help boost your creativity, alertness, memory, and even your immune system. And yet, too much might make it tough to focus. Similarly, some anxiety (a form of distress) related to paying the bills, for example, may energize you to focus on making money. Too little, and you're not motivated. Too much, and you're overwhelmed.

The objective is to make your stress work for you rather than against you. You want to have enough stress that it motivates you to keep making positive changes in your life, but not so much that it causes the physical, mental, emotional, social, behavioral, and even spiritual blockages that prevent you from being the optimal you.

So what is the "optimal" amount of stress?

It depends on the individual. Some people thrive under more stress than others. So it's important to figure out what's best for your unique self. Consider: Do you need a little fire under you to get moving? Were you the person who really did well pulling an all-nighter before a big exam? Or are you more motivated when you can focus on your underlying motivation for change, and start making progress that way?

Ultimately, to optimize your stress, you want lower distress levels and higher eustress levels.

Gauging Your Stress

If stress optimization is different for everybody, how do you know where you are? The key is to be aware of the cues that communicate *your* level of arousal.

Let's start with distress. Remember the Red Flags? They are the unpleasant emotions, physical sensations, and behaviors indicative of distress.

Personally, when I am in the Red Zone, I notice a lot of tension in my neck. And emotionally, I tend to feel frustrated and angry. As for behavior, I find myself getting annoyed with the people around me. Those are common Red Flags for me.

How about you? What happens when you're in the Red Zone of distress? What emotions, physical sensations, and behaviors show up for you? Identifying these symptoms is key to raising your awareness to your personal Red Zone and understanding how to get out of it. Whenever you experience any of these symptoms, you want to do something healthy and helpful to get yourself out of the Red Zone. We will explore specific strategies later in the chapter.

For now, let's look more closely at eustress, since it's the first step in optimizing your stress. To do this, consider the following scale. If you rate your eustress level at a zero out of ten, that means that you are not feeling any positive energy (excitement, passion, enthusiasm, joy). At this level, you may feel "blah" [a clinical term ;)]. In contrast, if you rate your eustress level at a ten out of ten, then you're feeling the most inspired, excited, delighted, zealous, exuberant, enthusiastic, and passionate you have ever been.

Low eustress levels might feel like boredom, disinterest, or mild depression. Your body might feel fatigued or lethargic. Behaviorally, you may procrastinate, sleep excessively, binge watch, incessantly scroll through social media, or lack focus. Now it's your turn.

What do you experience when your eustress is low (for instance three out of ten)? What emotions, physical sensations, and behaviors do you notice in yourself?

The goal is to become aware of your levels of distress and eustress so that you can ultimately optimize your overall arousal. How can you do that? When you notice high distress or low eustress, do something healthy and helpful to change those levels. Be proactive and reactive as needed.

The Best Kind of Mind-Control

When it comes to controlling stress, I highly advise taking a proactive approach. Each day, take steps to help get yourself into a better state of being. Some of my clients make a routine of this, scheduling a time for stress regulation every day. Others choose to implement stress-regulating strategies before events they expect will increase distress levels, such as before a presentation, speaking engagement, or interaction with a person known to cause conflict.

Before we look at specific strategies, let's look at how a proactive approach works.

Sarah realized she had a tendency to feel anxious when she worked with a certain colleague named Bob. He had a reputation for losing his temper, and she found herself walking on proverbial eggshells whenever he was around. That anxiety was unpleasant, and it interfered with her effectiveness as a leader. In our coaching session, Sarah shared with me how she got flustered when she noticed Bob's expression changing in meetings, indicating he was going to get angry. "When I see that look," she said, "I can't think straight." When her brain wasn't functioning optimally, she had a difficult time responding to questions or thinking strategically, which led to more signs of frustration in Bob. It became a downward spiral.

Something had to change.

Can you relate? Do you ever feel so stressed that you have trouble focusing clearly? Maybe it's difficult for you to remember things, process information, or communicate what you want to say. This is quite common. And luckily, we can do something about it.

For Sarah, by addressing her distress level proactively (that is, before she met with Bob), she noticed a significant change not only in how she felt, but also how she interacted with him. She told me, "He doesn't make me nervous anymore. And because of that, I can be more 'me.' I'm much more creative and a much better leader." Just last week, she told me Bob made a comment about how impressed he was with her work. That is the power of controlling your distress.

How can you proactively optimize your stress? There are countless ways. Here are a few ideas:

- Apply the "Magnitude of Gratitude"

- Get moving
- Get your "om" on
- Spend time with loved ones
- Laugh
- Go to bed
- Optimize your fuel

Let's briefly look at each one.

Apply the "Magnitude of Gratitude"

What if you could reduce the activity of the stress center in your brain so that it was not working overtime? Well, you actually can. You see, gratitude has been scientifically proven to cause changes in the brain, specifically reducing activity in the areas of the brain that control stress. No medication required. How cool is that?

Perhaps you've heard about a gratitude journal. It's a place where you document the people, experiences, and things about which you feel grateful. For some, this can be extremely powerful.

The key is to not only identify what you feel grateful for, but to also really experience the feelings of gratitude. It's the *feelings* that help decrease distress and increase eustress, not the list itself.

Here is how to make gratitude work for you:

1. Document at least three people, things, and/or experiences that you appreciate, and

2. Identify *why* you feel grateful for them.

For example, you might write that you feel grateful for your partner because you appreciate the love and laughter that you share. Or you appreciate your career because it affords you both income and a sense of purpose. Or maybe it's the cup of coffee you're consuming that brings you gratitude; it tastes amazing and offers you a delightful pick-me-up.

After you identify the "what" and the "why," take some time to bask in the gratitude. Close your eyes. Take a few deep breaths. And then picture the person, event, or thing that brings you gratitude. Sit in a place of appreciation. View yourself interacting with this person or enjoying the "thing" or experience. Really bring up the feelings of gratitude and savor this experience.

Sometimes the stress of life can interfere with us feeling gratitude. Maybe you are like some of my other clients who have trouble coming up with something that makes you feel grateful. Consider this question I posed in my book, *A Happy You: Your Ultimate Prescription for Happiness.*

> If you lost it all tomorrow, what would you miss most about today?

Would you miss: food, air, your loved ones, your home, or comforts you might take for granted (as we all do sometimes), like a hot shower or the ability to wiggle your toes? Going through the COVID pandemic offered a great opportunity to appreciate many things that we may have previously taken for granted, like hugging a friend or eating out at a restaurant.

Another method to consider: If an impoverished person from a developing country accompanied you for a day, what would they appreciate most that you take for granted? Perhaps it would be clean drinking water, or the freedom to choose your own friends and follow your own dreams. Maybe it's your closet full of clothes or indoor plumbing. Answering this question is a way to appreciate what you already have.

A few years ago, I was part of a group that sponsored 12 children from Africa to tour the U.S., singing at various locations. One of the kiddos was nine years old, and he was fascinated with the concept of a light switch. He spent over half an hour flicking the light switch on and off. On and off. His smile and fascination were almost palpable. *That's* appreciation. (By the way, when was the last time *you* appreciated electricity like that?)

Now it is your turn. Write out at least three things for which you feel grateful and why. Doing this daily can really help decrease levels of distress.

Get Moving

Exercise is a powerful creator and regulator of your energy. Sure, it can be a good way to lose weight and look great, but more than that, exercise is an incredible de-stressing agent that raises eustress levels. In fact, exercise has been shown to:

- Increase mood-enhancing neurotransmitters in the brain
- Enhance positive attitudes
- Release muscle tension
- Promote better sleep
- Have a calming effect

- Lessen anxiety and depression
- Increase mental focus
- Boost self-esteem (independent of how it can transform the way your body looks)

Any of those sound good to you?

Now, I used to *hate* to exercise. (Seriously.) I joked that it was "against my religion" to go for a run. Then things changed.

When I went to college, I was fearful of succumbing to the dreaded "Freshman 15" and decided that I needed to exercise. Not only was I going to exercise, but I was also determined to like it. So without realizing this was what I was doing, I rewired my brain (using what would later become Neuro-Retraining Training) so that I truly did—and do—enjoy it. In fact, I enjoyed exercise so much that for almost 20 years, I taught group fitness classes, such as kickboxing, step, spin, toning, etc.

How about you? Even if exercise isn't your favorite thing to do, the key is to find a way to move your body regularly. Find something you enjoy: dancing, playing with your children, cleaning, taking the dog for a walk, jumping on a trampoline, or playing a group sport—regardless of how "good" you are at it.

Don't have a lot of time? Avoid the all-or-nothing trap and try forging new pathways paired with positive emotion. No time for a full workout today? A five-minute walk is better than nothing and will feel good.

When you exercise, your mind and body both enjoy the benefits. Be proud that you're investing time and energy into a healthier and happier you.

Get Your "Om" On

When I was in graduate school for psychology, I discovered a wealth of research on the benefits of meditation. Meditation has been proven to:

- Decrease stress
- Control anxiety
- Boost happiness
- Improve attention and memory
- Generate kindness
- Reduce pain
- Promote restful sleep
- Increase self-awareness
- Enhance creativity
- Promote patience

I was amazed to discover all these benefits! Yet despite *knowing* this information, I didn't actually regularly practice meditation, because I didn't think I could.

Maybe you can relate. I would decide, "Okay, I'm going to meditate." I would sit in a chair, close my eyes, and start focusing on my breath. Then my mind would wander to all the things I needed to get done ("Call those three clients, study for my exam, go to the grocery store… Wait, what am I going to wear to the party this weekend? Darn, I better go shopping…"). When I realized my mind had wandered, I would try to pull myself back to my breath. I would think to myself, "Am I meditating? It doesn't feel like it. This isn't working. I'm no good at this." (PS: Did you catch the all-or-nothing thinking, there?)

After struggling for a few minutes, my mind would come to the conclusion, "I'm not meditating; I might as well take these 20 minutes to get stuff done." And that would be the end of my meditation.

Can you relate? A lot of people don't try meditation, or they give up on it quickly when they don't think they are doing it "right." I hear over and over, "I can't stop thinking about stuff." Let me share the truth with you: Even a monk's attention will wander during mediation. That's just the nature of the brain. So don't judge your ability to meditate in terms of whether or not you can keep your mind completely still. That only happens when your heart stops beating.

The simple truth is: Any meditation is better than none. Don't have 30 minutes to sit quietly? 15 minutes will do. Even five deep breaths are better than nothing (and that takes only a minute!).

Spend Time with Loved Ones (Fur Is Optional)

Despite how "connected" society is when it comes to "friends" on social media, we're becoming more and more lonely. Loneliness is not only stressful, it can lead to depression and even death. What's more, research indicates that loneliness is as detrimental to your health as smoking 15 cigarettes a day!

In contrast, spending time with positive people can help lift your spirits and eustress levels. Same goes for non-human loved ones. Even just a few minutes of playing fetch (with a stuffed bunny) with my dog Bailey gives me a positive boost of adrenaline.

Often, as adults, we prioritize career and family, while relationships outside of home and work get put on the back burner. For a life of True Success™, we must nourish relationships with family *and* friends. Time spent with them decreases distress and boosts eustress. Now that's a good investment!

So schedule time with people you love. Meet for lunch or coffee, go for a walk, or watch a show with a friend. Or even make new friends by taking a class, volunteering, or joining a group (like church, a gym, or a book club).

Laugh

We all love a good laugh, but it can feel like an indulgence. The truth is that laughter is a powerful de-stressing agent that has been scientifically proven to improve brain functioning. In fact, laughter stimulates learning, enhances creative thinking, and can even improve memory. It also helps us see events in a different, more positive light. Talk about staying out of the Red Zone!

Here are ideas for proactively staving off the Red Zone with humor:

- Make time with people who make you laugh.
- Spend less time with people who deplete your humor.
- Watch funny videos (I personally love hopping on YouTube to watch a quick clip from Ellen or James Corden).
- Listen to a comedian (Jim Gaffigan literally makes me laugh out loud alone in my car!).
- Sign up for a joke-of-the day text or email.

Sleep On It

Lack of sleep increases stress levels, depression, anxiety, pain, frustration, and anger. Sleep deprivation has been known to be an effective interrogation tool with prisoners of war because a sleep-deprived person has difficulty thinking straight. They're likely to spill whatever secrets they might have.

Ironically, millions of people willingly subject themselves to this torture. According to the CDC, one third of adults don't get adequate sleep.

In addition to the emotional toll of not getting quality sleep, sleep deprivation also impacts mental capacity. Forgetfulness, mental fog, the inability to pay attention, and trouble concentrating are all symptoms of sleep deprivation. While these sound like ADHD symptoms, they are also a result of not getting enough sleep, or enough "good" sleep. In fact, it's my strong clinical opinion that many of the medications for ADHD would not be needed if we all got better sleep!

"But I don't have *time* for sleep."

I hear this objection often from my clients, often. Here's the deal: Sleep deprivation decreases efficiency and increases distress. When you're exhausted, it takes you much longer to get stuff done, both physically and mentally. Therefore, by proactively ensuring that you get the sleep you need, you will actually have *more* time to do what you need—and want—to do.

Here are some ways to ensure you get your Z's:

- Prioritize sleep. Set a bedtime and stick to it.

- Develop a wind-down routine. This will allow your body to relax and learn when it is time for sleep. I usually dim the lights and read a bit to prime my body for sleep. Just like Pavlov's dog who salivated when he heard the bell because it had been paired with food, following a wind-down routine signals to your body: "It's time to sleep."

- Edit your sleeping conditions. Make sure your bed is comfortable, your room is conducive to sleep, and get rid of screens that can keep you up.

- Write yourself to sleep: Journaling before bed can be a great way to release any thoughts that might be keeping you awake and can serve as a way to prime your brain for more positivity. We will talk more about this in the chapter on priming your brain.

Optimize Your Fuel

Your nutritional intake has a huge impact on stress levels. What you eat regulates how you feel physically, emotionally, and mentally. A boost of sugar, for example, might give you some energy in the short-term but result in a crash when you come off the high. And then you may feel tired, sad, or stressed, and you may have difficulty focusing. Being hungry or thirsty can also negatively impact your mood.

Exploring specifics about nutrition is beyond the scope of this book. If you need help in this area, consult your doctor or another healthcare professional.

Make an Appointment

Like me, most of my clients are driven and ambitious. We do best when we have goals. So here's your assignment. Implement what I call a 3 x 5. Three times a day for at least five minutes, do something healthy and helpful to optimize your stress. Proactively identify what you are going to do and schedule it into your calendar. For example:

Time	Activity
6:00am	5 minutes of meditation
12:00pm	Go for a walk for ten minutes
10:00pm	Turn off screens and read a book with the lights dimmed before bed

With an intentional approach, you'll find that your stress levels start to equalize. You'll have a greater margin for those disruptions that might have otherwise sent you into the Red Zone.

When You Must React, Make It Productive

In the previous sections, we explored proactive ways to optimize your stress by decreasing distress and increasing eustress. Integrating these ideas into your day will help proactively keep your stress at optimal levels.

Sometimes, though, life happens, and you may find yourself in the Red Zone despite all that you are already habitually practicing. At those times, you want to take steps to reactively address your stress.

Specifically, if you notice your distress at a six or higher, do something healthy and helpful to change it effectively.

How? There's no one right way. I recommend that my clients develop a list of effective strategies that work for them. Why more than one? Because all actions won't be appropriate in all circumstances. For example, if I am onstage speaking to 2,000 people and my stress level is really high, I can't ask the audience to sit tight while I go take a bubble bath to lower my stress levels.

Here are some ideas:

- Meditate
- Listen to inspiring music
- Go for a walk
- Chat with an upbeat friend
- Pet your dog or cat
- Watch a funny video
- Jump on a bed
- Blow bubbles
- Pray
- Do push-ups
- Spend some time outside
- Draw or doodle
- Take a warm shower
- Go for a bike ride

Now it's your turn. Develop your own list of helpful ways to get out of the Red Zone. Keep this list with you—in your wallet, on your Smartphone, on your desk, or in your car. Whenever you notice yourself creeping into the Red Zone, react productively by taking action—do one item on the list. If that doesn't correct your stress level, try another until you feel your stress levels regulating.

Chapter Ten

Empowered Thinking: Helpful Self-Talk

My mini goldendoodle, Bailey, is napping at my feet as I write this. Most of the time, Bailey is a bundle of energy and love. And, as anyone with a puppy knows, he's a lot of work.

At night, Bailey sleeps in a crate. It's basically a Ritz Carlton-comfort level crate complete with a plush dog bed, soft baby blanket, and a chew toy, so for those of you who don't crate your dog, please don't think he is tortured in there.

This morning, I came downstairs, and I heard Bailey whimpering. When I opened the door to the laundry room, where his crate resides, I said, "Ugh! What stinks?"

It smelled like… feces.

Now, Bailey has been house trained since he was about three months old. This morning, however, he was having stomach issues and couldn't control his bodily functions.

So I took him out, made sure he was clean, and then started to clean the crate. When I didn't see any more poop, I threw the blanket and bed in the washing machine. I decided to let the crate air out. When I came back later, the stench was still there.

If I had returned his freshly laundered bed and blanket to the crate, hoping the smell would go away, I would have been sorely disappointed. Turns out, some excrement that I didn't see at first was hidden in the back of the crate.

Now, you may be wondering: What does Bailey's accident have to do with The Red Zone? (Stay with me here, I promise it will all make sense soon!)

Trying to think new thoughts without addressing the deep-seated ones can be like putting clean items into Bailey's crate when there is a big deposit of poop hidden in the corner. The smell will eventually overtake the fragrance of the laundered items.

This is basically what happens when we try to force affirmations. Consider: If you repeated, "I am a success," over and over again, yet you possessed the deep, fecal belief of, "I am a failure," your beliefs would not automatically change. You need to clean up or address the "mess" before you can rewire your brain.

Point, Counterpoint is a power strategy to help you do just that.

Point, Counterpoint

When you have an inaccurate, unhelpful thought, replacing it can be as simple as challenging that thought with authentic, true, and helpful thoughts.

Consider Keenan. He'd lost his job during the pandemic. He felt devastated and identified the belief (his deep-seated thought) that he was a failure. He needed to change this thought to change his circumstances. So we came up with some counterpoints to his automatic thought.

Automatic Thought	Counterpoints
"People will judge me."	"I am more than my job."
"I'm worthless."	"A lot of people lost their jobs."
"No one's going to hire me."	"My boss said I really did a great job, and she's hoping to rehire me when things get better."
"I'll never find a job as good as that one."	"If I were really being honest with myself, that job was not a great fit for me."
"This is the worst thing that could ever happen to me, I'm not going to be able to pay my bills."	"I am grateful for the severance and can now look for a position that's a good fit for me."

This works best when your counterpoints are accurate as well as helpful to replace automatic thoughts.

Avoid counterpoints that feel equally untrue. For instance, "I'm the most successful person in the world," would be rejected by the mind as BS.

Help for Creating Counterpoints

Sometimes counterpoints can be difficult to identify because you have held the automatic thought for so long and/or so deeply. So here are two strategies to help you create counterpoints that can be useful to you:

1. BFA (Best Friend Advice): If your best friend came to you sharing automatic thoughts that were exactly the same as yours, how would you react? If that thought was, "I'm such a loser," would you respond, "You really are. And not only are you a loser in this situation, but let me remind you of all these other times when you are a loser..."?

    Of course, you wouldn't say that to your best friend. Heck, you probably wouldn't even say that to someone you didn't particularly like. And yet that might be exactly what you're communicating to yourself. Instead, write out what advice or counterpoints you would impart to your best friend, and use those for yourself.

2. What would Jeff Bezos or Oprah do?: Think of someone you admire. This can be a mentor, family member, celebrity, person from history, or even a fictional character. What thoughts might your role model have when faced with the situation you're in?

Now it's your turn. Using a specific example from your life, identify an event that resulted in you feeling high levels of distress. Then determine what specific feelings you had, the thoughts that caused those feelings, any distortions that might have been present, and finally, the counterpoints to each of the thoughts that were not 100% accurate and helpful.

Harnessing the Power of Emotions

Counterpoints enter your mind via the conscious mind. Ideally, we want these new, more helpful thoughts to become so ingrained that the subconscious absorbs them, and they become automatic. For new information to enter the subconscious, we need extensive repetition coupled with emotion.

When a thought occurs at the same time as an emotion, that thought makes a deeper, more lasting impression. The more intense the emotion, the stronger the thought will be. Experiencing a strong emotion is like carrying a three-hundred-pound weight as you cross the field on your established path. Your heavier weight will forge even deeper tracks.

Consider Post Traumatic Stress Disorder (PTSD), for example. We know that suffering from a single traumatic event, laden with intense emotions, permanently rewires the brain (until treatment).

Knowing this, we can harness the power of emotions in a positive way—to help you rewire your brain for True Success™.

Now, consider emotions you would *like* to feel. Examples include:

- Joy
- Excitement
- Hope
- Gratitude
- Pride
- Confidence

- Enthusiasm
- Inspiration
- Love
- Admiration

When you repeat your counterpoints or new thoughts that you want to believe, really focus on your feelings that go with those thoughts. So for example, consider the thought, "I am proud of the success I have achieved so far and excited about creating even more success!" If this statement is true, helpful, and authentic, you'll not only accept it as true (versus rejecting it), the feelings will also cause your neuronal pathway to become deeper and stronger. The result? This thought becomes more automatic.

So identify the new thought you want to have and what feelings this thought conjures up. Then recite this out loud five times as if you 100% believe the statement, bringing up your desired feelings.

By forging new, consistent pathways in your mind, you can change your thinking and beliefs. This will allow you to make significant improvements in your personal and professional life, ushering in True Success™!

Chapter Eleven

Trigger Happy:
Anticipate to Participate

The brain, in its marvelous efficiency, has the capacity to recall information by way of memory tags we psychologists call stimuli. The smell of vanilla might provoke memories of Grandma's kitchen. The touch of velvet might elicit thoughts of luxury and the lure of power. The sound of church bells might conjure memories of wedding ceremonies. These evolutionary adaptations of the mind happen in big and small ways. Everyone has them. They can be sensory, or they can be people, places, situations, comments, actions, even our own physiology.

A trigger is just a shortcut to feelings or memories that, on the surface, may seem illogical. It can be hard to explain. In mechanics, a trigger is the mechanism that sets off a chain of events, like in a gun. A trigger can also be a wire that, when released, drops a bucket of cold water from the ceiling. For trauma survivors, some stimulus triggers act as shortcuts to highly undesirable emotions and memories. Avoiding the effects of that trigger is desirable.

In everyday life, triggers can impact our thoughts and lead to consequences (i.e., our feelings and behaviors). Some triggers themselves create distress on a Red Zone scale. Some triggers only activate when you're in or near the Red Zone, escalating existing distress.

It's important to note, however, that not all triggers are bad, and that some of the more challenging triggers can be used to help raise your awareness to your Red Zone.

What Triggers You?

Let's explore what triggers you in your life. In doing so, we'll be taking one step closer to getting you out of—and keeping you out of—the Red Zone. To follow are various examples of potential triggers. See if any of them ring true for you.

Are there certain people who, when you are with them (or even thinking about being with them), you notice your stress level creeping up? Perhaps a family member, (previous) friend, colleague, or another acquaintance? I worked with a client who, every time she had to interact with her ex-husband, found herself vaulting into the Red Zone. As a result, arguments were often the basis of their every conversation. Not only did this cause much distress for my client, but also her ex and their three children.

Are there places where you notice yourself feeling more stressed? Someone who is unhappy with their weight, for example, may experience distress when entering a health club filled with athletic-looking bodies or going to a bathing suit shop. I have worked with several clients who, when they return to their childhood home, say for a holiday, notice their stress levels rising.

Situations can certainly serve as triggers for many. Someone who is fearful of public speaking, for example, will likely notice an increase in anxiety when standing on stage in front of an audience. I worked with a client who was the CEO of a multi-million-dollar company.

She shared that while she felt extremely comfortable speaking in front of her team, customers, and even the media, it was when she was presenting to her board of directors that her stress levels skyrocketed.

Smells can be a trigger for some, because scent is the only sense that has a direct route to your brain. Odors can influence our emotions. Perhaps a smell from your past (such as an ex's cologne or perfume) can trigger you. One previous client was severely abused (physically and mentally) by his father when he was a child. His dad used to smoke about three packs of cigarettes a day. As an adult, the scent of cigarettes would put him into the Red Zone.

Painful memories can often serve as triggers. I was working with a client who was a professional athlete. By most people's standards, he was extremely successful, powerful, and strong. As a child, he was severely bullied for years by kids in his neighborhood. Just thinking about those harrowing encounters would throw him into the Red Zone.

Certain phrases can serve as triggers for some. One Sunday morning many years ago, my husband and I were in church. Our church at the time was a rather festive one where singing with passion was encouraged. Upon sitting at the end of the song, I remember whispering to my husband that his breath was not all that pleasant and offered him a piece of gum. Although he accepted the stick, I could tell he took offense to my attempts to help his breath. In all fairness, I was trying to be nice to those around us (and me) and was not trying to offend him.

The next Sunday, we were in a similar predicament, but I tried a new approach. This time, when I smelled his breath, rather than make a comment about it, I simply offered him a piece of gum. He smiled, accepted the stick, and thanked me.

After the service we went out to lunch at Mo's, a favorite taco place. I couldn't help but inquire why his reaction was so different (and much more favorable) this time. "I was saying the same thing to you," I pointed out. "I know," he said, "but for some reason it didn't offend me this time." Apparently, openly telling him he had bad breath triggered the feeling that I was judging him, but simply offering him a piece of gum (even though he *knew* it meant, "You have bad breath") did not trigger him. (Yes, you can imagine what it is like to be married to a shrink…)

Phrases that my clients over the years have identified as triggers include:

- You're just like your father/mother.
- You should lose weight.
- You're lazy.
- You'll never be as pretty as your sister.
- Must be nice to have won the genetic lottery.

In addition to what people say, their behaviors can also trigger us. Leaving during an argument, for example, can escalate distress in some people (even if the departure was meant to prevent escalation). Having your partner sitting and watching TV while there is housework to do is a common trigger for some. One client's distress used to skyrocket when witnessing their partner pouring an alcoholic drink because that often resulted in ugly, drunken arguments.

Specific sights and sounds can serve as stressful stimuli. Seeing injustices, pictures of places in your past when you experienced turmoil, the sound of someone's voice, or even songs (like that one you used to listen to over and over again when you were feeling down) may trigger your distress levels.

In addition, our physiology can serve as a trigger. Hormones, exhaustion, hunger, and pain can all increase distress. While the biological processes themselves can lead to increased distress, our thoughts can exacerbate the experience. People with chronic pain, for example, often spend a lot of time in the Red Zone. Unfortunately, this can lead to more issues, including depression, arguments with loved ones, and even greater pain. When working with those with chronic pain, I help them get out of the Red Zone, both in terms of decreasing their distress as well as changing their thoughts associated with the pain. "It will never get better" is a Red Zone thought that wreaks havoc in their lives. A belief that, "I am taking steps to control my pain each day," can really help them feel better.

Certainly, this isn't a complete list of events or experiences that can serve as triggers, but it is a foundation. Now, after reading the above, take some time to identify what your triggers are. Look back over your life (or at least the past five years) and determine themes from your past and present that send you into the Red Zone.

Why Do Triggers Escalate Distress?

While it may appear that triggers are the cause of distress, it is actually our thoughts about the trigger that are the cause of our emotional reactions. It's very important to drop the microphone into your brain to hear what you're telling yourself when a given trigger escalates your distress levels.

Consider Bill. Whenever his wife provided "feedback," it led to feelings of insecurity and even worthlessness. For example, one evening, after he loaded the dishwasher, his wife rearranged the dishes. This action triggered Bill's sense of inadequacy. "She thinks I can't even load a dishwasher correctly. She thinks I'm a failure."

Now it's your turn. For each of the triggers you identified, write out the thoughts and beliefs that you hold about them.

Empowered Thinking

The beauty about triggers is that they are personal. While we may think of them as external, in reality, they're all internal. They are our own judgments and fears. What's more, triggers offer great insight into what's really going on.

We cannot always change or control what others do or say, or what stimuli (such as sounds or smells) we experience. Those are often outside of us. What we *can* do, however, is change what is within us. We can take action to ensure that triggers help instead of hurt. If we're strategic, we can use our triggers to move from zones of distress into zones of True Success™. Here are three ways to do so:

- Check for Validity
- Name That Trigger
- Use the Trigger to Gain Valuable Feedback

Check for Validity

Identify the trigger that's sending you into the Red Zone and ask, "How true is the thought I have about this trigger?"

Here is an example from my personal life. When my husband and I first started dating, he came to pick me up at my apartment. When I answered the door, he said, "You look so comfortable." As someone who was dressing to impress, this assessment was a trigger for me. I thought, "Obviously he hates what I'm wearing and thinks I look awful." It caused me a lot of stress, which I'm sure I inadvertently shared with him.

After the third time he told me I looked comfortable (on three separate occasions), I asked him why he used that phrase. "I don't know, you just do," was his response. When I shared with him that, to me, that meant I looked dumpy and frumpy, he was genuinely surprised. "You look great," he said. "You always look terrific. Why in the world would you think that?"

So for three dates, I had been thinking he thought I looked bad, when in fact he thought I looked great.

Now, I respect that this may seem like a superficial trigger to some, but I'm human. Plus, I was 24 years old, lacking confidence, and I didn't have the tools I have today to question the validity of a thought.

How about you? What triggers can you explore to determine the validity of your beliefs about this trigger?

Name That Trigger

Sometimes simply calling out a trigger gives you control over it.

One of my triggers from my past is related to finances. Just the thought of looking at my P&L, reviewing where my income went, and setting a budget could send me into the Red Zone. Why? Because for decades, I held the belief that I could not make money. When in the Red Zone, propelled by this trigger, I avoided looking at my books or having conversations with my husband (who was very successful in business and could have been a great resource to my business). I would become less than pleasant when he even tried to offer assistance.

While I have taken steps to deactivate that trigger, it sometimes still comes up for me. So I now simply call it out. I proclaim, "Oh, that is my old money trigger creeping in!" (A good topic for another book!) When I do that, I take my power back. No longer is it in my subconscious, meddling with my emotions and causing procrastination. When I name it out loud, it goes into my conscious mind. And then I decide to simply notice it and move on.

Once we identify the trigger, we can actually *do* something about it.

Miguel got out of sorts when he saw that his kids weren't eating what was on their plates at dinnertime. Though he longed for a peacefully shared meal at the end of each day, he found himself snapping at them night after night. Upon reflection, Miguel realized that the trigger for him was simple: He was saying to himself that uneaten food signaled ingratitude for the hard work he did to provide for his family. So he decided to tell his children that the rule would be that they needed to say, "Thank you for dinner, Mom and Dad," before being excused from the table each night. This simple exchange helped everyone feel heard and accepted—and dinners were much more peaceful from then on. It worked like a charm!

How about you? How can you call out your trigger so that it no longer controls you?

Use the Trigger to Gain Valuable Feedback

Another empowering way to use triggers is to treat them like feedback. Instead of avoiding them, see them as a tool for getting what you ultimately want: True Success™.

When I was a kid, I loved going to the carnival. I looked forward to the rides (especially the spinning teacups), the food (funnel cakes!), and the games all year long. For years, I dreamed of winning a giant teddy bear at the fair, but my parents thought the games were a waste of time and money. So when I finally went to a carnival without my parents, I made a beeline to the game area to play Shock Wave. Do you remember that one? Players guide a metal loop wand over a wire from the starting point to the end. If you make it through without touching the wire, you win. If the wand touches the wire, a loud buzzer sounds, and the game is over.

I played this game until my quarters were all gone. Each time the buzzer went off, I made a mental note to correct my game the next round. "On that first twist, the wand needs to have more distance on the left side," for example. With my new-found knowledge, I forked over another 50 cents (yes, that was how much it cost back then) to play again. Each time I got farther and farther along thanks to the feedback I got from the buzzers.

What does this have to do with your triggers? Life is like a game. When you treat your triggers as feedback, you can better prepare for the next round. When you notice yourself getting triggered, stop and ask, "What can I learn from this? How can I use this experience to help me?"

Triggers can truly be a gift ("wrapped in strange wrapping paper," as my friend Darren Weissman says) but only *if* you use them. They let you know there is an issue that is impacting you—and you can take steps to deactivate that trigger.

Janon used to fly into the Red Zone when her husband said, "You're acting like your mother." Once she identified her trigger and used it as feedback, she knew his comment only hurt her when she let it. She taught herself not to get riled by that comment. Instead, when he made that comment, she recognized the attempt to push her buttons and get control (or feel like he had control) over the argument. So instead of reacting, she stayed rational and calm, avoiding the Red Zone altogether.

It won't happen overnight, but when you identify a trigger, you can take the steps to disable the power of that trigger.

Reacting to the feelings and thoughts in productive ways is key. Now, let's move into an even more proactive approach to the Red Zone.

Chapter Twelve

Stoked: Prime Your Brain for True Success™

It feels pretty good to know how powerful your brain is, doesn't it? We are literally wired for success in more ways than we can imagine. That's one reason I'm so passionate about my work. I love sharing with my clients how we can positively impact our own success!

In this final section, I want to show you how to get really proactive—before you even begin to find yourself in the realm of the Red Zone. Using these tools, you'll discover that you are stronger and can go even further with *minimal* distress and *maximum* success!

Remember when we talked about the subconscious versus the conscious mind? The subconscious, as efficient and helpful as it is, is kind of like a sponge. What happens when you submerge a dry sponge into water? It absorbs it, right? Now if you wring out that same sponge and put it into a glass of milk, what will it do? It will absorb the milk. A sponge doesn't say, "I don't do dairy." It just absorbs. The subconscious mind is similar. It absorbs information.

Sometimes this manifests in amusing ways.

What a Trip

Several years ago, I was speaking at a large event where Michelle Obama was also keynoting. Although she was no longer the first lady, she had a Secret Service entourage present with her. A few of us were permitted to meet Mrs. Obama and were escorted into a separate room with Secret Service agents all around. Michelle and a few of her staff were inside a tent-like structure (not the kind you camp in, more like a small room enclosed by fabric).

The rest of us were standing in a specific line according to our names. We had to leave our purses, phones, and any cameras in a secure area.

There were probably about 50 of us in line. While we were waiting for our turn, some of us struck up conversations. I posed the following question, "Who's someone you admire?"

People around me were sharing who they regard highly. When it was my turn to answer, I said, "One of the people I really look up to is Jennifer Lawrence. I love how comfortable she is in her skin; how authentic she seems. Remember when she went up to get her Academy Award and completely tripped? It didn't even phase her. I mean, talk about confidence and authenticity!"

A few moments later, it was my turn to meet the former first lady. I was so excited. The curtain to the tent opened. As I walked in, trying to be calm, cool, and confident, I literally tripped over my pink heels and was caught by none other than Michelle Obama herself. I would have completely face-planted otherwise. I imagined the Secret Service agents shouting, "Down, get her down, the lady in the pink shoes." Luckily, it was obvious that I was clumsy and not a terrorist. And Michelle was very gracious and didn't even acknowledge my ineptitude at walking.

Later, I thought about it. Why had I tripped? I have walked in heels for two decades and rarely trip and fall, but I had primed my brain by thinking about Jennifer Lawrence tripping to get her Academy Award.

Priming

Priming refers to using one stimulus to influence another stimulus. An example of priming is the soft pretzel restaurant at the mall that gives off delicious smells, enticing passersby to stop and grab a snack even if they weren't initially hungry.

In psychology, there are many examples of how one stimulus can impact our mood and actions. Simply saying, "I'm so stressed," or, "I'm too busy," can actually *increase* distress.

The bottom line? Our thoughts, feelings, and emotions can be primed by factors we're not even aware of, which greatly impacts our performance in other aspects of our lives. When practiced correctly and often, priming can help you cultivate positive emotions and drastically improve your quality of your life.

For our sake, we want to use priming for positive effects. Specifically, we want to take measures to get our mindset in a peak state so we can not only stay out of the Red Zone, but also exist in a state of passion. This will allow you to feel happier, enhance your creativity and problem solving, be healthier, enjoy better relationships, and even be more successful at work. Instead of saying, "I'm stressed," prime yourself for success. Flip it. Say, "I'm energized. I'm going to get a lot done!"

Put Priming to Work for True Success™

A great time to prime your brain is when you first wake up in the morning. You see, as you come out of sleep (as well as when you go into a state of sleep), your brain waves are in the alpha stage, operating around 10.5 waves per second. What that means to the non-scientifically inclined is that during this time, your brain goes into a very suggestible state. It's here that your subconscious is more impressionable.

So a great practice is to create a morning routine to be executed first thing in the morning. "Ugh, I hate mornings," you might be thinking. You will soon change your mind (pun intended!), because we are going to infuse your mornings with positivity. If you've been watching just three minutes of the news in the morning, reconsider that habit. It increases your chances of having a bad day by 27%. Think about that: Your subconscious absorbs information, and with the news usually being negative, that results in an increased likelihood of having a bad day. That's pretty powerful brain priming.

Consider taking five to ten minutes each day to positively prime your brain. It is a great investment that will pay off with big dividends. Just five minutes will help optimize your mindset for the day. Is having less stress, greater happiness, better relationships, and more success in your career worth five extra minutes in the morning? Yep! I thought so.

There are many ways to harness the power of priming. Here are some ideas. You will notice that some are consistent with ways to optimize your stress (there is a theme here):

- Meditate
- Visualize
- Journal
- Read or listen to something that inspires you
- Focus on gratitude
- Ask a question for which you want the answer
- Listen to music
- Laugh
- Exercise

Meditate

We explored the benefits of meditation in Chapter 9; making meditation part of your morning ritual can be a powerful way to prime your brain. You may choose to focus on your breath or repeat a mantra. Guided meditations are a great way to address a specific area of your life, such as improving health or increasing attention and focus. There are a bunch of apps out there that offer free or low-cost guided meditations. You can also download several free guided meditations referenced in the Resources section of this book.

Visualize

Take a few deep breaths and visualize something you would like to experience. It could be walking on the beach, enjoying success at work, or being confident in a previously stressful situation. When visualizing, don't worry about how it could happen. Just pretend as if it is happening. Enlist all of your senses: What do you see, hear, feel, taste, and smell? Visualize something that will elicit positive emotions such as gratitude, love, enthusiasm, happiness, and joy to really solidify the experience in your subconscious.

Journal

Journaling, or writing out what is on your mind, is a great way to start the day. You may choose to focus on gratitude, as we talked about in Chapter 9. Or perhaps you want to explore a specific topic, such as your intentions for the day about work, your happiness, or your relationships with others. Don't worry about spelling or grammar. Just write from your heart.

Read or listen to something that inspires you

Inspiring stories (such as autobiographies and biographies), podcasts, or TED talks can be a great way to prime your mind for the day. Simply listen while you are getting ready in the morning. This will provide a positive boost to start your day.

Focus on gratitude

We have talked about gratitude already, and I just want to highlight it one more time. Whether you journal about your gratitude or simply reminisce about it in your mind, really allow yourself to feel the feelings associated with gratitude. This is a very powerful way to feel happier and buffer yourself from getting into the Red Zone.

Ask a question for which you want the answer

Remember, your brain is like a sponge, especially when you first wake up. So if your first thoughts are, "How is this day going to suck?" or, "What is my boss going to do to annoy me today?" you're priming yourself negatively. Those are *not* questions for which you want the answer. And yet, if you ask them (even rhetorically), your subconscious will scour incoming data to answer them. Instead, ask questions for which you truly desire the response, such as, "How can I help out at least one person today?" or, "How can I use my gifts today to increase joy for myself and others?"

Listen to music

Music can powerfully alter your mood. Certain songs can elicit happiness, excitement, and inspiration, while others can elicit the blues. Develop a playlist of music that will enhance your energy in terms of beat, lyrics, and genre. Then listen to those songs to prime your mind for passion and not distress.

Laugh

They say laughter is the best medicine, and it certainly is a powerful way to prime your brain for the positive. Listen to a humorous podcast or joke around with your family. Laughing is a great jolt of positive energy to help start your day—no caffeine required.

Exercise

I affectionately call exercise "non-pharmacological Xanax." Moving your body is a great way to alter your biochemistry to release hormones, such as endorphins, that boost your mood. And the amazing thing about this is that it doesn't matter how you move your body. You can jump on the bed, dance around, go for a walk, do push-ups, sit-ups, play tennis—anything goes! So figure out what works for you (your body, interests, financial abilities, and time commitment) and start. Truly, even just a ten-minute walk in the morning can improve your mood all day.

As you get into the practice of continually checking in with yourself and directing your thoughts toward the positive, it will eventually become habitual.

Sometimes Going Deeper Actually Gets You Out

We have talked about the importance of getting out of the Red Zone so you can be the best possible you, and so you can let your inner light shine and dominate over your inner critic and overwhelming emotions.

And yet, there are times when going into the Red Zone—in a calculated way—can be helpful.

I don't know about you, but I can be really good at avoiding certain emotions that aren't comfortable. I often push them aside and try to focus on the positives, or I try to distract myself in an attempt to avoid them. Sometimes that can help you take control over your emotions rather than letting them take control of you. Sometimes, though, it can cause more problems.

I was working with a client named Emily. Emily was a mom of two middle schoolers, and she had returned to work after being a stay-at-home mother for years. On one hand, she wanted to go back to work. She longed for a sense of purpose outside of driving her children to their after-school activities, and she really enjoyed making money and feeling a sense of greater financial freedom. Yet part of Emily felt resentful. Despite going back to working outside the home, she still had all of her stay-at-home responsibilities. Sure, her husband Doug helped by going grocery shopping on the weekend, but the day-to-day home and child management still fell entirely on her, and she began to feel resentful.

This resentment came out occasionally. She was more irritable with the children, and she and Doug fought a lot more. Every time she saw Doug sitting on the couch in the evening when she was aware of how much still needed to be done around the house, she wanted to scream. And, despite trying to hold it together, she often did end up screaming at Doug, especially late at night when she was exhausted.

Right before Emily went back to work, her mother had died from cancer. Emily had been her primary caregiver, ensuring her mother's medical and every-day needs were taken care of. Needless to say, it was a very emotional time for Emily and her family. She was hoping that her new job would help her focus on doing something constructive where she could make a positive impact.

One night several months after going back to work, Emily just lost it. Her youngest informed her that he needed a trifold for a science project *tomorrow.* It was the proverbial straw that broke the camel's back. Emily found herself screaming and crying, convinced that her family took advantage of her. Emily was definitely in the Red Zone.

The thing about Emily's Red Zone, though, was that it was a theme that she had been repeatedly experiencing. Sure, she didn't yell every night at her family, but her underlying resentment came out at different times: when a child missed the bus ("What is wrong with you?!"), when she had no idea what to make for dinner ("Why do *I* always have to decide about dinner?"), and when she was exhausted but felt like she needed to get a few more items off of her "to do" list before collapsing into bed.

When you find a theme of Red Zone triggers and expe-riences, it can be an indicator that you actually need to work *through* the Red Zone. This does not mean you have a conversation with others when you are in the Red Zone. It does mean taking a look at why you keep going there so you can stop the pattern.

In working with Emily, I encouraged her to really identify what she was saying to herself when she was in the Red Zone. She identified thoughts such as, "No one respects me," and, "I'm a bad mother." She tapped into the resentment she felt and realized it was actually fueled by the sadness of missing her mom. Emily had not really mourned the death of her mother, having jumped right into a new job.

In really sitting with her emotions and thoughts, Emily was able to process them better. In working with me, she was able to work through the stages of mourning to help her get to a place of acceptance. She was also able to decrease the intensity of her distress, because rather than avoiding what was going on, she proactively dealt with her emotions.

Now, not everyone (thankfully) is dealing with the trauma of losing a loved one. And yet there are challenges that everyone has experienced (and COVID certainly added to those difficulties for many).

So if you find yourself consistently going into the Red Zone, you may want to consider taking some time to really let yourself process whatever it is that keeps sending you there.

How? Talking it out with a close friend or working with a coach or therapist can certainly be helpful. Another option is writing it out.

There is a concept in psychology called "written emotional disclosure," which is another name for journaling.

Dr. James Pennebaker, a psychologist I greatly admire, was really the pioneer in this area. His studies usually consisted of randomly assigning groups to either write about something mundane (such as what they did the day before) or write about their deepest, darkest trauma or struggle.[6] Participants usually wrote for about 20 minutes on three to four different occasions. And that was it. They were then followed over the course of a few months. The findings demonstrated a decrease in distress, such as depressed mood and anxiety, as well as fewer health issues and even improvements in their immune systems.

Why did participants receive these benefits from journaling difficulties? While we don't know the exact mechanism, it appears to be that working through their thoughts and emotions allowed the participants to release their distress. In essence, it allowed participants to process their thoughts and feelings so that these entities could no longer control them or propel them into the Red Zone.

You can use this technique, too. Schedule out a 20-minute block of time when you will not be disturbed. Write out what's really bothering you—the events, your thoughts, and your feelings. Don't worry about spelling, grammar, or even making sense. Just put the information from your brain onto the paper. Repeat this exercise two to three more times on other days and reap the benefits of going deeper into the Red Zone so that you can eventually get out... and stay out.

Conclusion

By now, I hope you're empowered with the knowledge that when it comes to your life, you're in the driver's seat! Even if your life has previously been a pattern of bouncing from one Red Zone to the next, you can change your life *now*.

It starts by taking ownership.

By learning to identify the slides in your projector and understanding the role your thoughts play in determining outcomes, you're on the right path. You've learned to identify the faulty lenses that can distort thoughts. And, thanks to the efficiencies of the human brain, you've learned to throw off unhelpful biases. You've learned to harness triggers to use them for good. And finally, you've learned to prime the mind to proactively ward off the Red Zone.

Getting out of the Red Zone is an integral part of True Success™. This concept has grown from my work with clients for over two decades, many of whom came to me as super "successful on paper," yet something was missing. Filling that void with more money, more achievement, extravagant vacations, new homes, living vicariously through their children, getting into a new relationship, or other external changes didn't work.

Starting sometime in their adulthood, a false expectation was set: "If X happens (I make a million dollars, land my dream job, find the love of my life… etc.), *then* I will feel successful." Once that milestone is achieved, however, they end up replacing X with something else that they believe will get them to the place of fulfillment.

"Success" becomes the proverbial treadmill—forward movement without actual progress.

Maybe you can relate. Perhaps you thought you'd find satisfaction once you landed that promotion, got married, had children, got divorced... you name it. Maybe you've even experienced contentment for a bit. But that feeling was temporary.

Well, I am here to tell you that what you desire is within reach. In fact, I have developed the True Success™ Formula to help you achieve just that. What is the True Success™ Formula? Simply put, it's this equation:

Passion x Purpose x People

By *Passion*, I mean positive energy—an optimistic mindset even during difficult times.

Purpose refers to finding or creating meaning in your life.

Whereas the *People* component speaks to the fact that we are social beings. Optimizing relationships brings greater connection and joy.

In *Get Out of the Red Zone*, we've examined Passion by way of dealing with its enemy: The Red Zone. In future books, we'll dig into the other two factors: Purpose and People.

For now, I hope you feel empowered to move forward and optimize your success with passion and a greater understanding of how your brain works and what you can do to get out of—and stay out of—the Red Zone!

Appendix

But wait, there's more! This is the resources section, where I get the opportunity to share with you how you can discover even more.

First, please know that I am so grateful that you have read this whole book (although I recognize you may be like my oldest daughter and her grandmother—it might be genetic—who reads the last pages before fully jumping into a book. And if that is the case, you are absolutely welcome here regardless).

Second, independent of how you arrived here, I want to share with you some additional resources to help you get **out** of the Red Zone to transform your stress and optimize True Success™. These are available at ElizabethLombardo.com/GetOutOfTheRedZone and include:

- Resources to help you work through some of the exercises presented in this book
- Guided meditations to help you get out and stay out of the Red Zone
- Information about a biological mechanism that can provide objective feedback on when you are in the Red Zone (What?!)
- Lastly, information on how to take the next step to truly get out and stay out of the Red Zone so you can be the person you want to be, have the happiness and fulfillment you deserve, and create a life you truly love

You deserve to have less distress. You deserve to live a life outside the Red Zone. And so do your family, your loved ones, your colleagues, your friends, and everyone else who interacts with you.

YOU can be the catalyst for positive change in your life and, as a result, in the lives of all of those around you. Distress can be infectious, but so can happiness. In fact, research in positive psychology shows us that when you are happier, not only are the people around you happier, but so are the people around them. There are two degrees of separation (at least) when it comes to positive energy.

So stop settling for average. Yes, most people are stressed. It's time for you to make the powerful decision to get out of the Red Zone, to transform your stress and optimize your True Success™.

You are not alone. I am here for you. I gratefully welcome you on this journey to help us all get out of the Red Zone. This book is merely the beginning of your new life.

Until next time!

—Dr. E

Acknowledgements

There are so many amazing people in my life who I appreciate dearly.

When I applied to psychology schools, I had no real idea what I was doing. For some reason, Dr. Arthur M. Nezu saw potential in a truly psychologically clueless applicant. I am forever grateful for this trust in me and the incredible training he provided me. Another mentor has recently appeared in my life: Steve Hall. Thank you, Steve, for your generosity in helping a struggling small business owner. Your wisdom and support are truly gifts.

I often describe my writing as a Charlie Brown Christmas Tree. It has the roots and the main structure but can use some prettying up. And that is exactly what many people have helped me do, including my fabulous publisher and dear friend, Martina Faulkner, Tyler Asman, who is a wealth of information, Winter Murray (Go GA!) and the rest of the team at IOM, and editor-extraordinaire, Ami McConnell. Thank you all!

Thank you to my team, including Patty Dominguez, Charlotte Day, Maja Kazazic, Rabecca Gaspard, and Derek Warburton, for all that you do to help us get this important message out there! And to the EleVive coaches: Tom Cardamone, Amy Cardamone, Steve Drum, and Kelsey Schwab. So excited to be teaching teens how to get out of the Red Zone!

To my friends and family who (usually) keep me out of the Red Zone, I am eternally grateful. This includes Elisa Allen, Carrie and Dave Gaston, Julie Schwan,

Teri Albus, Lisa Potash, my sister, Martha Moreau, and my incredible mom and dad. And, of course, thank you to Jeff, Kelly, and Grace for your unconditional love and helping to motivate me to be a better wife and mom.

Notes

1. All client names have been changed throughout the entire book to respect anonymity.

2. For the ease of explanation, certain biological processes discussed in this book will be simplified. If you are looking for an in-depth assessment of what is taking place neurocognitively, please look elsewhere. ☺

3. https://www.cnbc.com/2020/04/06/coronavirus-is-taking-a-toll-on-workers-mental-health-across-america.html

4. https://hbr.org/2011/06/the-happiness-dividend

5. https://www.ncbi.nlm.nih.gov/pubmed/7475659

6. https://psycnet.apa.org/record/2019-26569-005

About the Author

A licensed clinical psychologist and coach, Elizabeth Lombardo, Ph.D. is on a mission to help people get out of their own way to create a life they love. Dr. E (as her clients affectionately call her) is a regular media contributor to outlets such as the *Today Show* and *Good Morning America*. She lives outside of Chicago with her husband, two daughters, and four-legged son.

Made in the USA
Middletown, DE
17 March 2022

62828216R00089